Management for Professionals

The Springer series *Management for Professionals* comprises high-level business and management books for executives. The authors are experienced business professionals and renowned professors who combine scientific background, best practice, and entrepreneurial vision to provide powerful insights into how to achieve business excellence.

More information about this series at http://www.springer.com/series/10101

Martin Hofmann

A Holistic Approach to Process Optimisation

Tools and Practical Examples to Create Efficient Workflows

Springer

Martin Hofmann
Zug, Switzerland

ISSN 2192-8096 ISSN 2192-810X (electronic)
Management for Professionals
ISBN 978-3-658-34096-4 ISBN 978-3-658-34097-1 (eBook)
https://doi.org/10.1007/978-3-658-34097-1

This Springer imprint is published by the registered company Springer Fachmedien Wiesbaden GmbH part of Springer Nature.
The registered company address is: Abraham-Lincoln-Str. 46, 65189 Wiesbaden, Germany

'Indeed, many business processes contain the potential for optimisation. When you hold this book in your hands, you have already taken an important step. In this book, you will receive simple, clear and feasible instructions on how to develop low-waste, sustainable and competitive processes for your company. It is crucial that you do this together with your employees. I wish you every success with it!'

Markus Bertschi, Lean Six Sigma Master Blackbelt, Facilitation & Consulting

Preface

Advancing globalisation and the rapid technological progress of recent years are strongly shaping our economic environment and leading to ever more rapid change. Thanks to new technologies, customers have access to new shopping channels 24 hours a day, 7 days a week! As such, new digital possibilities and ways to create and distribute their products and services more quickly and efficiently are opening up to companies.

This rapid change means that work processes in companies no longer remain stable over a long period of time and have to be constantly revised instead. This is one of the reasons why various methods of improvement management are being used more and more. These methods have their origins in the production sector, where they have been successfully applied for a long time. Increasingly, however, they are also being used to improve work processes outside of production.

Yet simply copying the approach from the production sector and applying it to the administration does not usually lead to the desired success, as the necessary holistic orientation and the required framework are often lacking. The basis for the continuous improvement of work processes is the corporate culture defined and exemplified by the company management with the corresponding framework conditions. Only when this is anchored in the company and lived by all those involved, the various methods with the corresponding tools can be used effectively and sustainably.

This book provides the necessary theoretical basis and ensures its transfer into everyday life. In the first part of the book, the basics are taught; the reference to practice is established in the second part.

Detailed structure of the book:

Part I: Basics

Chapter 1: Vision of Efficient Processes
As an introduction, the history and vision of the ongoing improvement and more efficient design of existing workflows are highlighted.

Chapter 2: Prerequisites and Framework Conditions for a Successful Improvement Culture
This chapter deals with the prerequisites that must be anchored in a company in order to establish a successful improvement culture.

Chapter 3: Process Improvement Methods
The most important methods for improving work processes are presented and contrasted.

Chapter 4: Tools for the Optimisation of Workflows
The most common tools from the methods discussed in the previous chapter are presented and their applications explained.

Chapter 5: Influence of Digitalisation on Process Optimisation
This chapter focuses on the increasing influence of digitalisation on the ongoing optimisation of existing workflows.

Part II: Practice

Chapter 6: Putting Process Optimisation into Practice
Concrete examples from practice are used to illustrate how improvement projects can be successfully implemented in everyday life.

Chapter 7: Simulations to Illustrate the Improvement Methods
Finally, several simple simulations are presented, which are used in teams and groups for team building and for a better understanding of efficient work processes.

In addition to conveying the theoretical basics, it is my particular concern with this book to pass on concrete experiences from my everyday professional life to the readers by means of practical examples.

In order to give even more weight to this aspect and to emphasise the reference to the daily challenges in particular, two interviews with experts are included in the book. *Stephan Spada* deals with the optimisation of work processes aided by the Kaizen method on a daily basis in his professional work and is therefore very familiar with the topic and the requirements. *Kateryna Brönnimann* successfully accompanied the development and testing of a new maturity model.

Enjoy reading the book and applying it in practice.

Zug, Switzerland
July 2021

Martin Hofmann

Contents

About the Author

Martin Hofmann is an expert in accounting and controlling and completed an EMBA with a specialisation in Controlling & Consulting as well as training as a Six Sigma Green Belt. He has several years of experience in process management and as a leader of improvement projects.

Part I

Basics

1 Vision of Efficient Processes

The Need for Efficient Processes
The constant change in the economic environment of a company has a strong impact on existing processes and workflows. It is shown how a company can react to this and keep its processes up to date and what benefits this produces.

The History of Improvement Management
In the last century, various improvement methods were developed, such as Kaizen or Six Sigma, which are geared to the needs of the customers and aim at a continuous and sustainable optimisation of the work processes. The historical development and the influential personalities are briefly described.

Value Creation and Waste in Administration
Identifying and eliminating waste in work processes is an essential starting point for increasing efficiency. This chapter explains the terms 'value creation' and 'waste' and shows how they can be identified in everyday life.

M. Hofmann, *A Holistic Approach to Process Optimisation*, Management for Professionals, https://doi.org/10.1007/978-3-658-34097-1_1

1.1 The Need for Efficient Processes

In a continually changing environment, there is a need for ongoing adaptation to altering circumstances, for example, increasing internationalisation, new technologies such as the Internet or the development towards digitalisation. Those who do not adapt to these new conditions will have difficulty orienting themselves and holding their own in a progressively complex environment. For example, it is becoming increasingly difficult to move in our society without a smartphone.

Just as it happens to every individual in his or her personal environment, companies are also forced to constantly adapt to new circumstances and to make their processes and workflows more efficient in order to survive in international competition and to be able to satisfy the changing needs of their customers.

Definition Term: Workflow A workflow is a chain of activities to achieve a defined goal. Accordingly, no distinction is made as to whether information or materials are the subject of the process (definition according to Brenner 2018).

The optimisation of processes can be implemented either continuously in small steps or in a larger innovative leap. In continuous improvement, existing processes are analysed and made more efficient based on the experience gained. This results in a constant optimisation in small steps. In contrast, an innovation—for example, a new technology—is a one-time major development step. Figure 1.1 shows the interplay between continuous improvement and leaps in innovation.

The mindset of consistent improvement is not new. Humans have always tried to make their lives as easy as possible. For example our ancestors, who constantly refined their hunting methods, or the sailors who built ever-more robust and faster ships to journey across the seas.

With industrialisation occurring in the nineteenth century, systematic methods to make processes more efficient first found their way into the modern economy. At

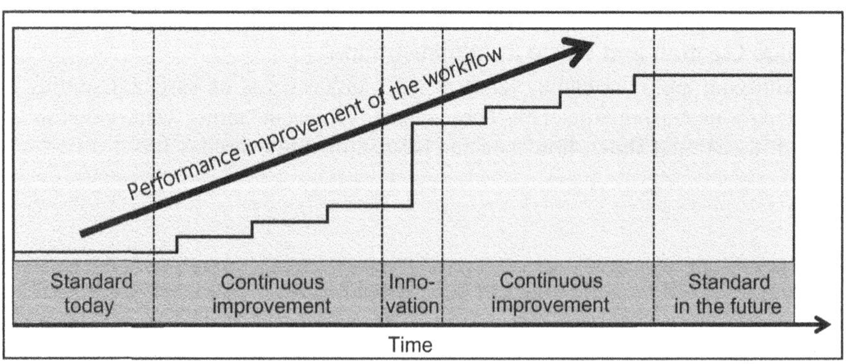

Fig. 1.1 Continuous improvement versus innovation (based on Schmelzer and Sesselmann 2013)

that time, the challenge was to produce enough products to satisfy the large demand. Therefore, the focus was primarily on making production more efficient.

Today, it is no longer enough to produce enough goods; they must also meet the particular individual needs of the customers so that they can be sold. Thus, the focus is much more on the customers and their needs. This also means that the entire processes from receipt of the order to receipt of payment are the focus of the more efficient orientation and no longer just the actual production.

1.1.1 Benefit

The ongoing optimisation of work processes with a focus on customer needs results in products and services that meet customers' wishes and needs even better. This results in the company achieving higher sales, more satisfied customers and a stable basis for long-term and sustainable development. Figure 1.2 summarises the main advantages.

Ideally, the benefit of the customers and the benefit for the company are in a positive relationship; this means that both, the customers and the company, benefit at the same time. However, it can happen that interests conflict with each other and that both cannot be satisfied. For example, this can be the case with unusual customer wishes that cannot be fulfilled with the existing structures. In these cases, a clear corporate strategy serves as a guideline that defines the orientation and focus of the company's range of products.

In the past, the company could determine the selling price based on costs plus a profit mark-up. Nowadays this is hardly possible, as the customer has the choice between different suppliers with similar products and services. He usually chooses the products or services that meet his needs the most accurately and are available at a competitive price. Thus, the selling price is strongly dependent on the market and the prices of similar offers. The profit on a product or service is thus equal to the selling price minus the actual costs. Figure 1.3 shows that optimised operations influence this equation and increase the company's profit.

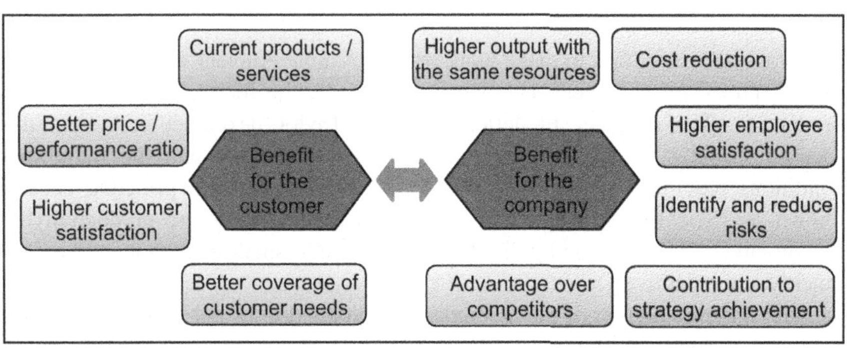

Fig. 1.2 Benefits of ongoing adjustments to processes

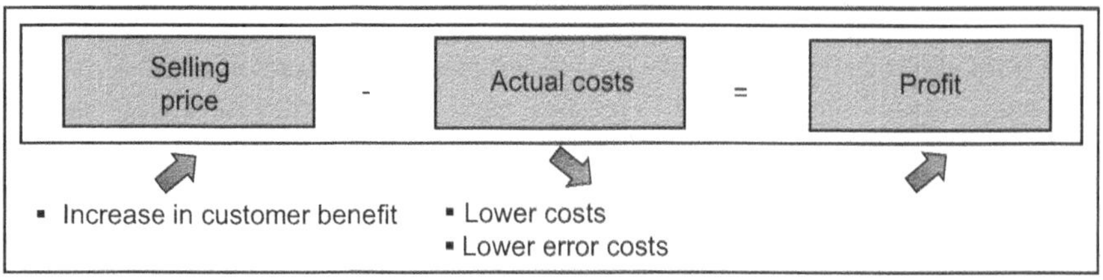

Fig. 1.3 Impact on the company's profit

Thanks to optimised processes, the products and services are better adapted to the needs of the customers. It may even be possible to cover additional customer wishes with the existing products. This can be seen, for example, in mobile phones, which contain more and more additional functions. This leads to customers being willing to pay more. The sales prices can be raised accordingly.

With the constant optimisation of processes and the elimination of waste, costs can be reduced. Furthermore, the error rate is lower with optimised processes, which in turn results in lower costs and higher customer satisfaction. It is crucial to always focus on the needs of the customer when adapting the processes to create a product or service. Creating a product or service that is not in demand is a waste and therefore without any value.

It is essential that not only certain details within the processes are analysed but that the entire process from receipt of order to payment and delivery is considered. If only certain details are optimised, while it may lead to selective improvements, it can also negatively impact other aspects of the process. According to Brenner (2018), when one considers an optimal process, all activities are coordinated from start to finish, unnecessary steps and waste are eliminated, and the lead time is as short as possible. Also, according to Schmelzer and Sesselmann (2013), it is necessary to pay as much attention to effectiveness as to efficiency. Efficient actions do not equate to being effective. It is crucial to do the right things the right way.

1.2 The History of Improvement Management

The first systematic steps to make work processes more efficient were taken as early as the end of the nineteenth century. At that time, the focus was on optimising production. The engineer Frederick Winslow Taylor developed a system that focused strongly on the standardisation of work processes and the framework conditions required for this (compare Taylor 1998). Taylor's principle became known as 'Scientific Management'. This means increasing the productivity of human labour. This is done by dividing the work into small units that can be done quickly and repetitively.

With the introduction of the assembly line production in 1913, Henry Ford was the first to introduce the approach on a large scale, pursuing the goal of producing an affordable car for everyone. Thanks to this process approach, he managed to greatly

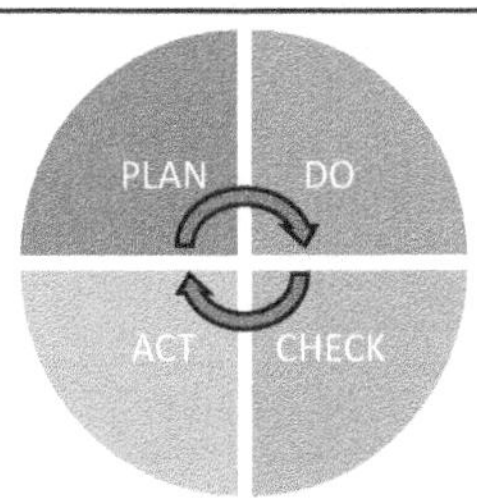

A central element of process management is the PDCA cycle or the so-called "Deming circle", which describes the phases of continuous improvement. It is named after William Edwards Deming, a pioneer of quality management. The abbreviation "PDCA" stands for Plan - Do - Check – Act. The circle shows the four steps according to which, as stated by Deming, changes should be processed. Many methods for improving processes are based on this model.

Fig. 1.4 The Deming Circle (based on Deming 2018)

reduce the cost of production while at the same time increasing output. With the introduction of industrial manufacturing and the associated mass production, quality assurance became an increasingly important issue. This gave rise to the Deming Circle approach, which is illustrated and described in Fig. 1.4.

Henry Ford's concept was further developed by Toyota in Japan after World War II and consistently integrated into the corporate philosophy. The goal was to completely eliminate waste in the processes. Like the Ford model, the Toyota production system is based on the flow of labour. However, Taiichi Ohno at Toyota went a step further: While they were concerned about the storage of parts in the Ford system, Toyota eliminated the warehouse as much as possible with the just-in-time approach. In addition, Taiichi Ohno placed great emphasis on the continuous development of processes. This approach became known as Kaizen.

In the 1990s, Bill Smith, an American engineer and scientist from Motorola, developed the Six Sigma method. Again, there are many similarities with earlier methods. The main difference, however, is that Six Sigma includes an essential mathematical component, which is used for the systematic measurement of deviations and trends. At about the same time, business reengineering emerged, which takes a more radical approach and, instead of aiming for further development of processes, aims for new development. Figure 1.5 shows the chronological overview of the most important milestones in the development of improvement management.

1.2.1 Influential Personalities

In the last 150 years, there have been various entrepreneurs and scientists who revolutionised work processes with their visions and a cooperative business model. The most important of these are:

- **Frederick Winslow Taylor** (1856–1915)
  - Founder of process management
  - Introduced work preparation
- **Henry Ford** (1863–1947)

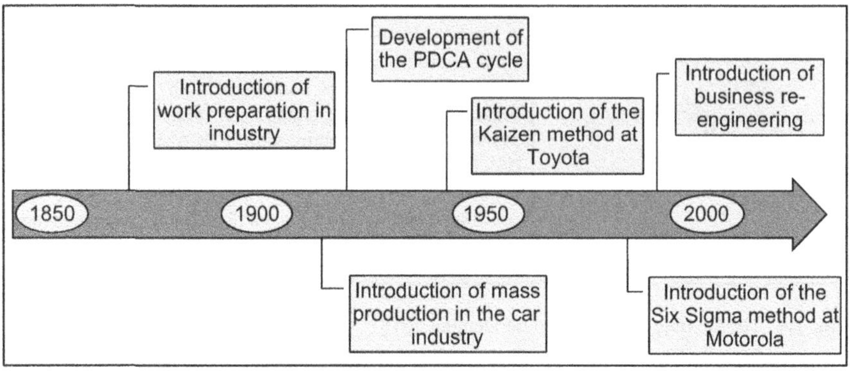

Fig. 1.5 Milestones of improvement management

  - Developer of mass production
  - Strong increase in production
- **Kiichiro Toyoda** (1894–1992)
  - Founder of the Toyota Motor Cooperation
  - Success thanks to continuous development
- **William E. Deming** (1900–1993)
  - Pioneer in process and quality management
  - Founder of the PDCA Circle
- **Taiichi Ohno** (1912–1990)
  - Developer of the Toyota Production System
  - Founder of Kaizen
- **William Bill Smith** (1929–1993)
  - Engineer at Motorola
  - Developer of Six Sigma together with Dr Mikel J. Harry

Even though these entrepreneurs came from different parts of the world and lived in different eras, they drew inspiration from each other. For example, Kiichiro Toyoda travelled to America to study the car industry and the approaches of Henry Ford before he started producing cars in Japan.

1.3 Value Creation and Waste in Administration

When looking at waste, it is important to not only scrutinise the actual defective products and inadequate services but to examine the entire process in detail. In doing so, it is also important to harmonise divergent goals. In the Kaizen method, according to Ohno (2019), the following three terms are distinguished in this regard: Insufficient standardisation and rationalisation create waste (muda), inconsistency (mura) and overburdening (muri) in work processes, which ultimately lead to the production of defective products.

1.3.1 Value Creation in Administration

Work processes consist of several steps and individual activities that are necessary for the creation of a product or service. The individual activities should provide a value-adding contribution to the end product. However, this is often not the case. There are activities that constitute an obvious waste. These typically include activities such as searching for required documents or filing the same documents several times. Furthermore, there are numerous activities with hidden waste, which do not generate any direct added value as well. These include, for example, printing out documents for monitoring or long distances between the different workplaces in the team.

▶ **Definition of Terms Used**

▶ **Value Creation** These are all activities that add value to the product or service. In other words, they are activities for which the customer is willing to pay because they receive added value for their money.

▶ **Waste** These are all activities that do not add value to the product or service and for which the customer is not willing to pay as he does not receive any equivalent value in return. Waste can be divided into two sub-categories: hidden waste and obvious waste.

▶ **Hidden Waste** The first sub-category of waste is hidden waste. Although these activities do not add value, they cannot simply be dispensed with under the given circumstances. Otherwise, the product or service cannot be created. Examples of hidden waste are setting up or transport.

▶ **Obvious Waste** The second sub-category of waste is obvious waste. This includes all activities that are obviously not necessary to create a product or service. Obvious waste includes, for example, rejects, rework, overproduction or waiting times.

In improvement management, the identification of waste provides valuable information for increasing efficiency in existing work processes. The goal is to quickly eliminate the obvious waste through targeted optimisations, to make the hidden waste visible and to reduce it as much as possible. However, this does not mean that value-adding activities do not contain potential for improvement and should not be considered in the context of improvement projects.

In order to make the added value and waste in a workflow visible, the individual activities are divided into the groups described above. The following simplified example of a shoe purchase in a specialised shop is intended to illustrate this.

First, let's consider what the customer wants. In this example, they wish to buy a pair of new shoes that look smart and fit their foot perfectly. To do this, they go to a specialist shop for advice. This advice adds value to the shoe purchase because it

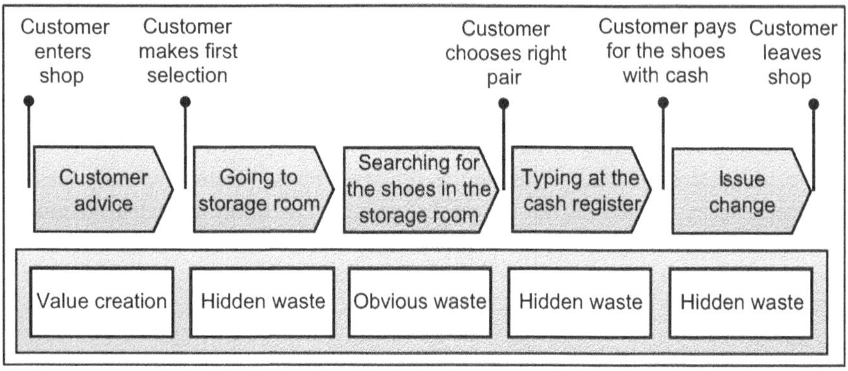

Fig. 1.6 Value creation and waste in the workflow

helps the customer find the right pair of shoes for them. After the first selection of possible shoes, the shop assistant has to fetch them from the storage room. This activity does not add any value from the customer's perspective, so it is considered a hidden waste. Let's assume that there is a mess in the storage room and the right pair in the desired size has to be found first, which constitutes an obvious waste. Finally, the payment for the shoes is also a hidden waste that does not add any value from the customer's perspective and has no impact on the appearance or quality of the shoes chosen.

The easiest thing to eliminate is the obvious waste. In this example, it is sufficient if the existing shoes in the warehouse are stored and labelled correctly. The hidden waste is more difficult to deal with. It does not represent any added value for the customer, but seems to be necessary for organisational reasons, as not all shoes in all sizes can be stored directly in the shop.

Figure 1.6 shows the process of the shoe purchase described in the example, including the classification into value creation and activities involving waste.

The rapid technical and economic change with the increasing digitalisation and the growing importance of the Internet as well as the stronger internationalisation of markets has had a massive impact on the shoe industry in recent years. In the example shown, this opens up new possibilities for increasing added value and for more efficient processing of a shoe purchase in a specialist shop or via the Internet. On the other hand, this change also entails existential risks for the established market participants, as new players with new business models are entering the market.

1.3.2 Waste in Administration

According to Taiichi Ohno, the founder of the Toyota Production System, there are a total of seven types of waste that must be identified and eliminated in order to achieve a real improvement in the efficiency of work processes (compare Ohno 2019). Although Taiichi Ohno was primarily referring to waste in industrial production, the seven types of waste can also be found in administration, as the following compilation shows:

- *Too many work steps:* Instead of directly entering the work reports into the computer system, they are often filled out by hand in a first step and only then transferred to the system. This leads to unnecessary extra work, time delays and additional sources of error.
- *Movement:* When paying for consumption in a restaurant by credit card, the waiter goes back to the counter and retrieves the card terminal before continuing the payment process. This leads to additional distance covered and a time delay.
- *Inventory:* Business cards are still very important in everyday business, which is why several boxes are usually ordered at once. However, these are no longer of much use if the employee's function in the company changes after a few months and new ones have to be ordered. This leads to useless inventories that have to be disposed of.
- *Transport:* The work reports of all plumbers working in the field, filled out by hand, have to be sent to the head office for monthly billing. This delays invoicing and causes additional postage costs.
- *Overproduction:* For the monthly project meeting, all existing documents are printed beforehand and sent to all the participants. To be on the safe side, additional copies are procured for the meeting. This leads to an overproduction of unneeded documents and a higher time expenditure for preparation.
- *Repairs/errors:* The wrong telephone number was printed on a newly designed hotel flyer by mistake. Either the wrong number has to be pasted over manually on all flyers or the flyers have to be printed again. This leads to high rework costs.
- *Waiting times:* To create weekly turnover statistics for all sales locations, the basic data per location is downloaded from the central sales database. The download of the necessary data per location takes several minutes. This leads to unnecessary waiting times and a higher expenditure of time.

Causes of Waste in Administrative Workflows

In addition to the seven types of waste that originate in production, specific causes of waste can be identified for administrative work processes. Brenner (2018) divides these into the following main points:

- *Interfaces:* If information or documents are passed on between people, departments or systems, numerous interfaces arise. Often, the focus is on departments rather than workflows, and there is no clear definition of what needs to be passed on to whom and in what form. This can lead to additional waiting times, queries and errors.
- *Information loops:* If the required inputs for a pending activity are incomplete or incorrect, it results in unnecessary information loops. Additional queries and time delays are some of the consequences. Furthermore, the number of possible sources of error increases.

- *Sub-optimisation:* If individual employees try to change and optimise their activities in the work process without involving the others, it can be to the detriment of the entire work process. This can result in higher overall costs and breaks at the interfaces.
- *Roles/responsibility:* In the workflow, it is often not clearly defined who has to complete which activities by which deadline. This results in additional waiting times because no one feels responsible for the further processing. In the absence of deadlines, there is also a lack of time orientation.
- *Sequential flow:* The individual steps of a workflow are usually carried out one after the other, although they could sometimes be handled in parallel. The additional waiting time during the workflow leads to an extended processing time, which in turn can lead to a delayed creation of the final product or service.
- *Too many approvals:* In administrative workflows, multiple signatures and approvals are often required to ensure correct processing. These are sometimes redundant and unnecessary. This results in a higher time expenditure, duplications and increased waiting times.
- *Doubled information:* The same data is entered into different systems. If it is not ensured that the exact same data is available in the different systems, this can lead to errors. In addition, the workload for data entry and reconciliation of the systems increases.
- *Shadow systems:* Employees keep informal systems, such as their own Excel spreadsheets or files, although the same information and data are already available in the official system. The redundant databases often cause errors in the workflow.
- *Lack of transparency:* The processing of a customer's application was started days ago. The current status of the processing and the person responsible are unknown. In addition, it is not possible to predict by what date the application will be completed. This leads to unnecessary waiting times, errors and duplications.
- *One way for everything:* If only one workflow exists for all cases, this leads to unnecessary work steps for certain cases (example: re-entering the billing address even if it is identical to the delivery address). The result is additional revision of already existing data and unnecessary waiting times.

Capacity, Productivity and Utilisation

A key focus in the continuous improvement of work processes is on capacity and productivity, as well as optimal utilisation. Eliminating waste and non-value-added activities has a positive impact on both of these parameters.

► **According to Brenner** (2018), **these terms are defined as follows:**

► **Productivity** Productivity measures how many units of a specific output were produced in a given period of time. For example, in the customer service department last Friday, a total of 125 enquiries were responded to by the 5 employees present. This corresponds to 25 enquiries per employee. The calculation is based on the formula shown in Fig. 1.7.

$$\text{Productivity} = \frac{\text{Output}}{\text{Input}} \quad \text{or} \quad \frac{\text{Output quantity}}{\text{Input factor}}$$

Fig. 1.7 Calculation of productivity

▶ **Capacity** Capacity refers to the possible output of a workflow. In the example of customer services, the 5 employees can jointly answer a maximum of 160 enquiries in a working day of 8 h and an average processing time per enquiry of 15 min. This corresponds to a maximum of 32 enquiries per employee. The central question about capacity is: How much can be achieved with the available input?

▶ **Capacity Utilisation** The utilisation rate measures the effective output of the workflow in relation to the capacity. In the example of customer services, this is 78.1% (answered customer requests of 125 over the maximum capacity of 160 customer requests).

High-capacity utilisation is essential for the economic production of the service. However, high-capacity utilisation also harbours dangers. For example, an unforeseen increase in customer enquiries leads to bottlenecks in customer services, and it is no longer possible to answer all enquiries promptly. This in turn leads to dissatisfied customers.

Defining the output in administrative processes is sometimes quite complex, as the output is more difficult to define than in industrial processes and it is usually more difficult to standardise. For example, individual customer enquiries can be of varying duration depending on the request, and thus the processing time also varies greatly. Nevertheless, it is necessary to be able to determine these variables as precisely as possible in order to optimise the processes.

▶ **Recommended Reading** To delve further into the beginnings of industrial production and thus the beginning of improvement management, I recommend the book *My Life and Work* by Henry Ford (2007). The book gives a fascinating insight into Henry Ford's vision and shows how he managed to implement it.

References

Brenner, J. (2018). *Lean administration: Verschwendung in Büros erkennen, analysieren, beseitigen*. München: Carl Hanser Verlag.

Deming, W. (2018). *Out of the crisis*. Cambridge, MA: Massachusetts Institute of Technology.
Ford, H. (2007). *My life and work* (reprint originally publ. in 1922). New York: Cosimo Classics.
Ohno, T. (2019). *The Toyota production system*. Productivity Press.
Schmelzer, H., & Sesselmann, W. (2013). *Geschäftsprozessmanagement in der Praxis: Kunden zufrieden stellen, Produktivität steigern, Wert erhöhen*. München: Carl Hanser Verlag.
Taylor, F. (1998). *The principles of scientific management*. Mineola, NY: Dover Publications (Originally published: New York: Harper, 1911).

2 Prerequisites and Framework Conditions for a Successful Improvement Culture

Prerequisites for Optimising Workflows
In order to anchor a sustainable improvement culture, the corresponding prerequisites and framework conditions must first be established. The question as to which framework conditions are crucial for success and why anchoring them in the corporate strategy is imperative is answered.

The Procedure for Implementing Improvements
A clear structure and a targeted approach enable the greatest possible improvement. It is shown which phases are undergone and how a sustainable effect is achieved.

Limits of Improvement Management in Administration
Not in all situations can the desired effect be achieved by optimising work processes. Here is shown, where the limits lie.

M. Hofmann, *A Holistic Approach to Process Optimisation*, Management for Professionals, https://doi.org/10.1007/978-3-658-34097-1_2

2.1 Prerequisites for Optimising Workflows

It is human nature to strive for continuous improvement. The vision to work as efficiently as possible and to focus on the needs of the customers is prominently listed in many companies' mission statements. Nevertheless, many companies struggle with the continuous development of their work processes.

It often seems more promising to scrap existing workflows and start from scratch with far-reaching restructuring measures and the involvement of specialised consultants. In particular, the continuous optimisation of existing workflows takes a great amount of time while still only inducing minor progress, at least in the short term. However, the radical methods often lead to a considerable loss of know-how, a higher error rate and therefore more customer complaints. This is where the advantages of continuous improvement lie. It leads to fewer interruptions, which ensures the stability of work processes and the continuity in the company. In addition, continuous improvement increases employee and customer satisfaction.

However, many companies fail to introduce continuous improvement management because their necessary framework conditions for a successful implementation are lacking, and thus no sustainable improvement culture can develop. Figure 2.1 shows the necessary conditions that must be established and lived in a company for a successful introduction.

At first glance, these prerequisites for optimising work processes do not appear to be anything out of the ordinary, and successfully establishing them seems relatively easy. However, this first impression is deceptive, as these necessary foundations can only be established with prudent and comprehensive corporate management, as well

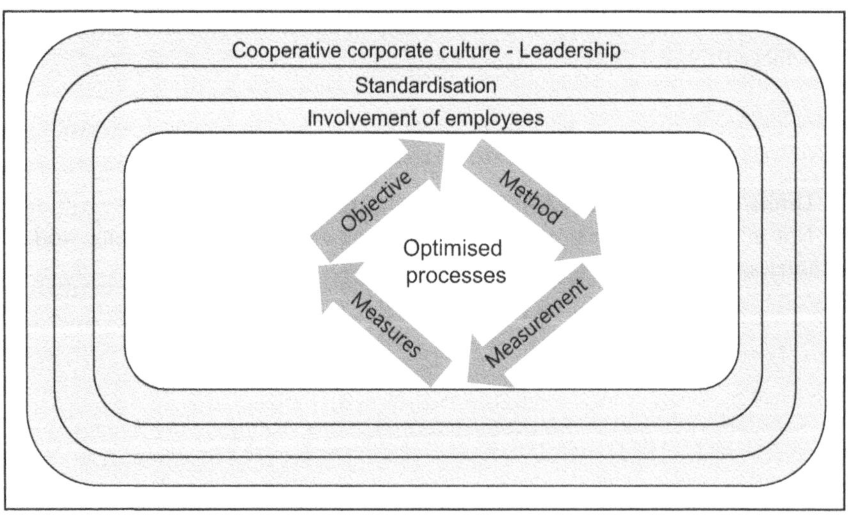

Fig. 2.1 Prerequisites for optimising workflows

as the inclusion of all stakeholders. Moreover, the consistent anchoring of these values in the corporate culture requires a great deal of time and patience.

As these prerequisites and framework conditions for optimising workflows are crucial for successful implementation, they are described in more detail below, and the concrete contents are illustrated.

2.1.1 Cooperative Corporate Culture: Leadership

The absolutely most important framework condition for establishing and maintaining successful improvement management is a cooperative corporate culture. This includes all values, norms and attitudes that shape the decisions, actions and daily behaviour of the members of the organisation. Such a culture is shaped particularly by the following characteristics:

- *Company purpose:* Creation of products and services that are geared to the needs and wishes of the customers and are constantly being developed further. Great importance is attached to long-term and sustainable development.
- *Attitude towards employees:* Employees as people are the centre of attention. They are being actively involved in the future development of the company, and their needs are taken into account in all decisions. Employees are actively encouraged and an active learning culture is promoted.
- *Dealing with conflicts and mistakes:* Conflicts and problems are actively addressed. Decisions are communicated transparently. Mistakes are made visible in order to learn from them and to continuously improve work processes.
- *Dealing with change:* Change and transformation are addressed and tackled at an early stage. All internal and external stakeholders are actively involved in the change process.
- *Continuous development:* Existing work processes are continuously optimised and developed with a focus on customer needs. This is done in collaboration with the employees.
- *The customer is in focus:* The internal work processes are designed with a view to the final product, or, respectively, the final service and are oriented towards the wishes and needs of the customer.
- *Communication:* Open and direct communication is maintained with all stakeholders, including detailed information about the goals set and the method of their achievement. It is important that the basis for decisions and motivations can be illustrated and communicated. For the communication of long-term developments, strongly visualised central notices have proven to be very effective.
- *Leadership by example:* The applicable internal company values and norms are exemplified and consistently applied in everyday life by the entire management and all executives.

Essential for a successfully lived corporate culture is the mindset of all those involved. This means that the culture must be supported and lived by both, the leadership and all employees. According to Brenner (2018), managers have a role model function in designing efficient processes, so that the attitude and behaviour of the entire workforce can develop towards a culture of improvement.

2.1.2 Standardisation

Continuous development is based on existing work processes. This means that the currently existing processes are analysed in detail. In doing so, each individual work step as well as the entire process is examined for optimisation possibilities. For this to be possible, a stable and standardised starting point is needed first. Only then can existing problems be recognised and waste be identified. In the absence of standardised processes, these must first be worked out and recorded. Only then can further development and optimisation begin.

Standards bring a certain stability to the work processes. They are described and anchored with detailed documentation and clear checklists. In addition, these standards with their respective documentation help to better absorb short-term staff absences and substitutions and to avoid mistakes. Think about your own work situation for a moment: Do you know what you would have to do if your colleague were to be absent tomorrow due to illness? Do you know the tasks that need to be done and how to do them? Do you know where the most important documents are stored? Do you know the significant contact persons?

It is important that the existing work documentation and checklists are always up to date and correspond to the work processes lived in reality. I have often heard the following statement: 'Oh, you know, it is actually laid down this way, but we do it quite differently here'.

2.1.3 Involvement of Employees (Know-How)

Continuous development of work processes without the involvement of the employees concerned is doomed to failure from the outset. Not even hiring highly decorated external consultants is of any help in that case. The employees who take care of the daily tasks know the existing problem areas best and are aware of the difficulties in everyday life. It is crucial to create the appropriate platforms that promote exchange between all those involved and allow space for change. This could be, for example, an internal suggestion system. After all, it is the employees who implement and live the new processes—or not. It is therefore important that they support and understand the changes.

In addition to the provision of these platforms and their ongoing operations, the company management itself is required to ensure the necessary know-how regarding the common improvement methods and their implementation. It is important that this know-how is broadly anchored and promoted internally in the company.

2.1.4 Objectives/Methods/Measurement/Measures

Once the framework conditions have been established in the company and are being lived, the actual improvement of the processes can begin. The procedure is based on the Deming Circle (see description in Chap. 1) and the four phases (plan, do, check, act). The content of these four phases is described as follows:

- *Objective setting (plan):* To design work processes more efficiently and to develop them further, it is essential to first set clear objectives regarding the desired results. On the one hand, this applies to the overall goals at the company level (e.g. with annual goals), and on the other hand, it is also applicable to the concrete and measurable objectives for each individual planned improvement project.
- *Methods/tools (do):* The established methods and numerous tools help in the concrete development and implementation of the individual improvement projects. It is essential that know-how regarding their application and implementation is available. Ideally, the company is setting up its own team of specialists. These specialists ensure methodological competence, train the employees involved and manage the upcoming improvement projects. The most important improvement methods and the most helpful tools are presented in detail in Chaps. 3 and 4.
- *Measurement (check):* Measuring the achievement of objectives is an important check to prove effectiveness and sustainability. It is carried out together with all the participants after the completion of each individual improvement project. At the same time, as the achievement of objectives is being measured, a review of the implemented optimisations is performed. A measuring of target achievement at the company level is also conducted periodically.
- *Measures (act):* The results of the target achievement control and the findings from the review serve as the basis for the definition of targeted improvement measures to optimise the work processes further. The measures taken due to all the measurements and reviews are again incorporated into the objective of the future continuous improvement of the work processes and thus close the circle of effect. This ensures sustainable development of the overall system at the company level.

2.2 Procedure for the Implementation of Optimisations

After anchoring the framework conditions described above, the next step is to make the processes more efficient by implementing concrete improvement projects. Here, it is crucial for the overall effect that not just any uncoordinated ideas are tackled indiscriminately. Instead, it is more promising to have an overarching and coordinated orientation of the planned activities.

Figure 2.2 shows the individual phases from the idea for improvement to its implementation and the measurement of the results achieved. Phase 1, which is

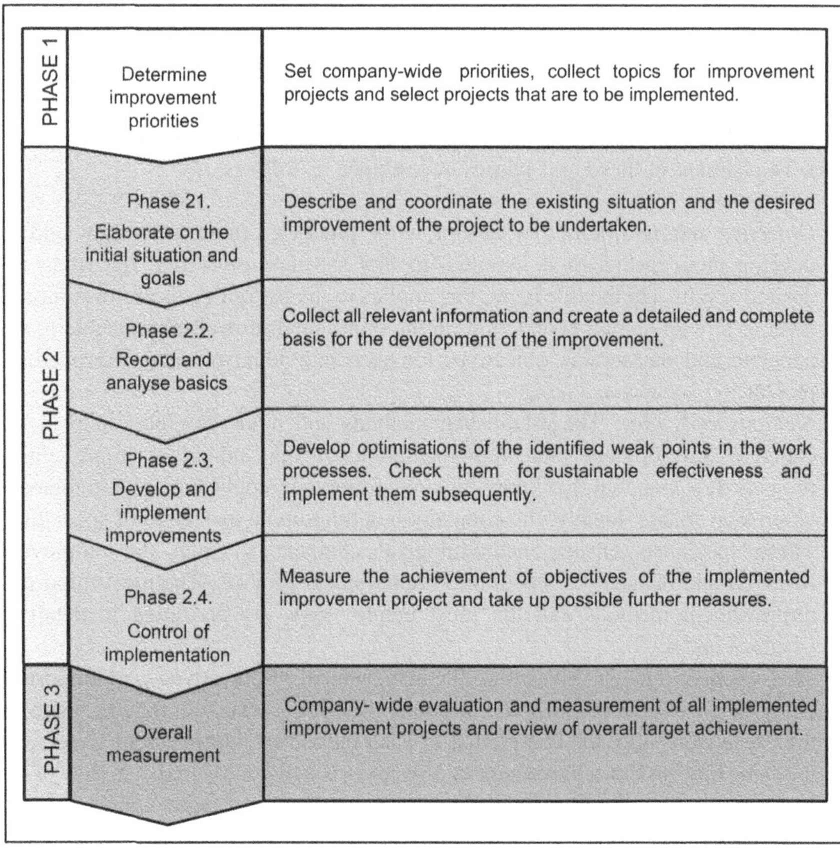

Fig. 2.2 Phases of improvement (based on Brenner 2018)

effective company-wide, starts out with the definition of the focal points and the selection of the individual improvement projects. The improvement projects chosen in that phase are then tackled and implemented individually in the second one. Finally, in the third phase, the achievement of objectives is measured across the entire company while taking into account all the optimisations that have been tackled and implemented. The findings of this last phase can lead to further or new improvement projects, which are incorporated into the first phase in the next run.

On the following pages, the three phases shown are elaborated on, and the individual components are considered in detail.

2.2.1 Phase 1: Determining the Improvement Priorities

A company-wide and jointly coordinated approach is essential for successful improvement management. The holistic orientation enables the setting of

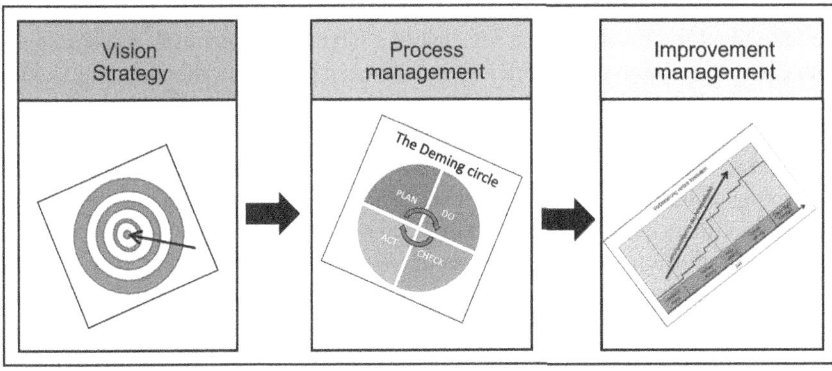

Fig. 2.3 Link between strategy and improvement management

overarching focal points, which are based on the corporate strategy and thus contain the central fields of action. In addition, the individual improvement projects can thus be coordinated, and duplications can be avoided.

It is important that overarching goals are set at the beginning of this phase, as they facilitate the selection of individual improvement projects. In addition, the defined goals provide the basis for measuring the achievement of objectives after the implementation. Caution: Not only monetary goals should be defined but also non-monetary goals that increase customer and employee satisfaction, for example.

The definition of the overarching focal points and the aspired goals normally takes place once a year. This allows for stable planning of resources, as well as overall coordination with the annual goals and with the corporate strategy. However, a shorter rhythm is also conceivable.

Alignment of the Improvement Projects with the Strategy

Projects that make a direct positive contribution to the strategic priorities are particularly effective. For this reason, it is important to check the improvement projects against the corporate strategy. This is done through process management, which ensures the link between the improvement project and the strategy. Process management ensures the control, implementation and monitoring of work processes. Figure 2.3 illustrates this link between improvement management and strategy.

Additional improvement topics can also be derived from process management; these result, on the one hand, from the operation of the individual processes (inputs from the process owners and the affected users) and, on the other hand, from the measurement of the process indicators (deviation from the target values).

Setting the Priorities

It is very important that improvement projects are not launched in an uncoordinated manner and that optimisations are not performed on a large number of processes at the same time. On the one hand, this would overload the organisation, and, on the other hand, it would lead to duplications and unstable processes. It is important that the individual improvements are selected in a targeted manner and are coordinated with each other. From my experience, the five-step procedure shown in Fig. 2.4 has proven to be helpful in practice.

My experiences from the past years have shown that it is very important for the later implementation of the chosen topics and focal points that the decision-makers are involved at an early stage. To achieve this, a short workshop with the responsible company or division management is particularly suitable. The aim of this workshop is to select the improvement projects to be implemented from the collected suggestions for optimising work processes and to initiate their implementation.

To ensure a common understanding of the proposals to be assessed, I recommend, as an introduction to this workshop, to briefly present the collected and described topics as well as the overarching focal points derived from them and to discuss their content together with the participants. Afterwards, steps 4 (assessing topics) and 5 (selecting topics) take place together with the leadership team.

For the consistent further processing of the selected topics, it is very important that a sponsor from the participating management body is designated for each selected improvement project. With the designation of a sponsor, the support of the management in the processing and implementation of the improvement topic is ensured. This makes it possible to react promptly to any difficulties that arise at any stage.

2.2.2 Phase 2: Implementation of the Individual Improvement Projects

After the improvement projects to be implemented have been determined along with the responsible management, and a sponsor has been assigned to each topic, the second phase comprising the actual improvement of the work processes begins. This is usually done in collaboration with the employees involved, either with a workshop or with a project. The implementation phase is divided into the following four sub-phases:

1. Elaborate on the initial situation and goals.
2. Record and analyse basics.
3. Develop and implement improvements.
4. Control of implementation.

The implementation of the improvement project should be led by an experienced facilitator. With their experience and methodological competence, they play a decisive role.

1)Collect topics

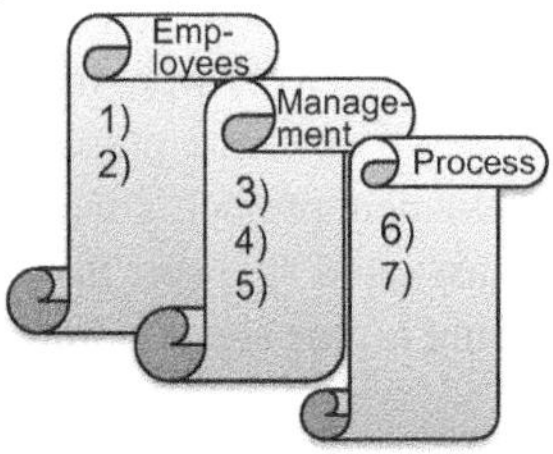

The first step is to identify possible topics for improvement. These can stem from a wide variety of sources, such as derivation from the strategic focal points, or inputs from process owners or employees. It is important that the selection of topics is as broadly supported as possible, so that all essential topics are covered.

2) Delineate topics

Topic	Description	Participants
1)		
2)		
3)		
4)		

In the second step, all previously identified topics are formulated in detail for better classification. The following points are essential: comprehensive description of the proposed topic, expected benefits, urgency of implementation, qualitative and quantitative goals, expected expenditures for implementation as well as naming of the staff involved.

3) Set priorities

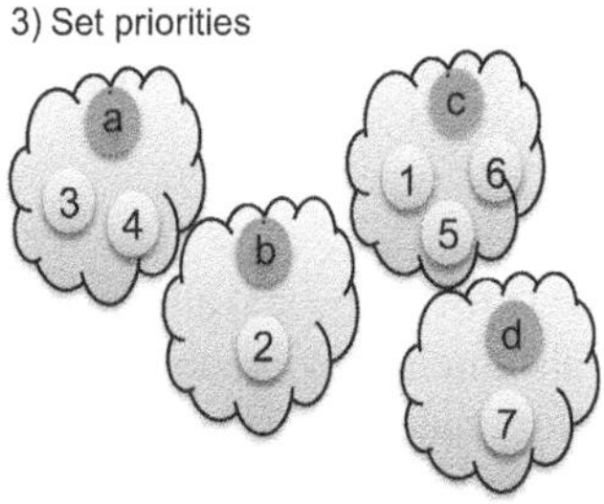

The next step is to check whether the individual independent proposals of topics can be grouped into overarching focal points. It may well make sense to assign sub-themes to the individual focal points. The formation of focal points is conducive to a focused and targeted approach and avoids unnecessary duplication.

4) Assess topics

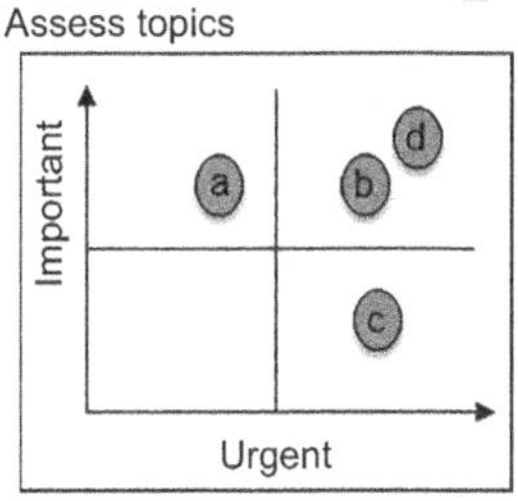

In the fourth step, the individual topics and thematic priorities are evaluated and rendered comparable. The uniform evaluation enables the prioritisation of the different suggestions for improvement. The Eisenhower matrix is a particularly suitable tool for this (see the description of the "Eisenhower-Matrix" tool in chapter 4). Thus, the evaluation is based on the criteria of urgency and importance.

5) Select topics

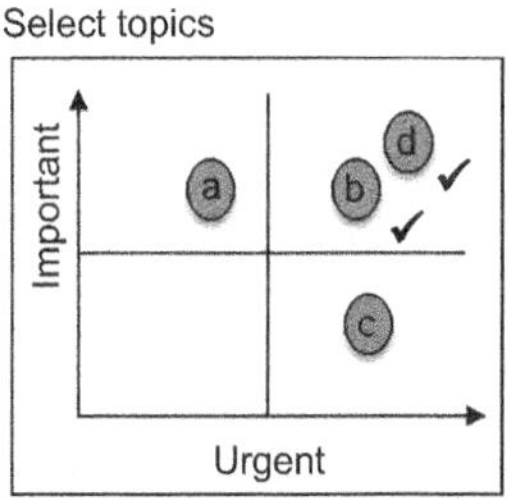

In the last step, the topics and thematic priorities with the highest importance and the highest urgency for implementation are selected. It is important that the topics not selected are not simply forgotten. Instead, it would make sense to collect them in a theme repository and keep them ready for future optimisations.

Fig. 2.4 Choice of topics for improvements

(1) Elaborate on the initial situation and objectives

In the first phase, all the ideas for improvement that were discussed were briefly described, and the expected benefits as well as the desired objectives were defined. This basis must now be further delineated and refined as we enter the preparation phase for the processing and implementation of the improvement project. This step is carried out jointly by the responsible facilitator and the assigned sponsor. If necessary, the employees concerned are involved. The following topics are elaborated in detail:

- Initial situation/problem description
- Delimitation
- Effect/goals
- Involved parties
- Implementation (place, time and duration)

To determine these points, it makes sense to create a Fact Sheet. This provides a clear structure and enables a systematic approach. By signing the Fact Sheet, the sponsor also shows his support for the implementation project. The description of the tool 'Fact Sheet' is included in Sect. 4.1.2.

(2) Record and analyse basics

If the workflow to be processed has not been described sufficiently or at all, this must be redressed. This is done in collaboration with all employees involved in the process, as they know best about the current situation and the challenges ahead. According to Ohno (2019), it is very important that this recording of the actual process takes place at the location of the event. He uses the Japanese term 'Gemba', which stands for on-site observation. Only this on-site observation ensures that the recorded activities also reflect the effectively lived work process.

In contrast to work processes in production, processes in administration are less visible and therefore more difficult to grasp. Therefore, it is even more important that the work processes are recorded in a complete and detailed manner at the beginning of the improvement project in order to make the waste visible.

The recording of the actual workflow forms the basis for determining the problems that currently exist. In addition, other important information such as the evaluation of key figures or feedback from customers is consulted. Next, fields of action are defined and described in detail for all the problems.

(3) Develop and implement improvements

After identifying and describing the main fields of action, the next phase is to discuss possible solutions and concrete improvements together in a team and to elaborate and describe them in detail. Various tools and aids for a structured procedure are available for this purpose. For a description of selected tools, see Chap. 4. The procedure for implementing an improvement is shown in Fig. 2.5.

Just as it is crucial that the recording of the actual process takes place directly on-site, the same holds true for the development of solutions. In most cases, it is not

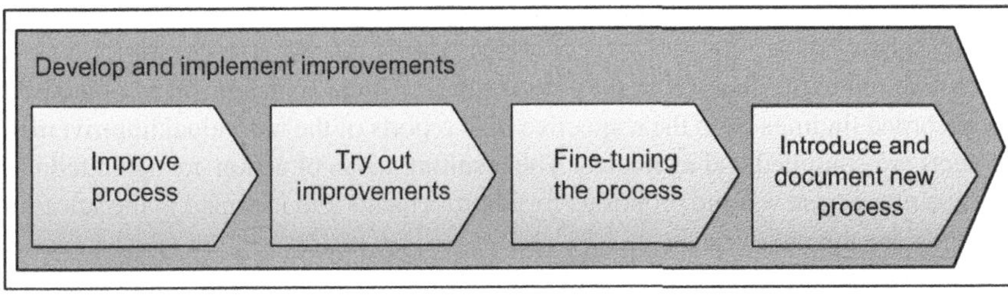

Fig. 2.5 Procedure for implementing improvement projects

enough to analyse and work on the recorded fields of action from a distance in an air-conditioned meeting room in order to develop practicable approaches to improve them. It is important to observe and experience the relevant activities live on-site under the actual working conditions. This is the only way to get an overall impression of the need for action and the suitability of the possible proposals for improvement. The adjustments decided upon should be implemented as soon as possible and also immediately on-site. This way, possible weak points can be recognised quickly and remedied in a direct manner.

In order to be able to sustainably anchor the adjustments to the workflow and to prevent a relapse into old habits, it is important to quickly implement the measures decided upon and to communicate and document them accordingly.

(4) Control of implementation

After the completion of each individual improvement project, the effect of the adjustments made is to be reviewed again in detail. At the same time, it must be assessed whether the previously set goals have been achieved and whether any new problem areas may have arisen in the workflow concerned. It is also important to check whether the innovations have been documented properly and are being implemented accordingly. The optimisations achieved and the findings from the final review are summarised in a final report. This report is discussed with the sponsor and the management team and then distributed to the positions defined.

Ideally, this final review is carried out in collaboration with all those involved a few weeks after the improvement project has been realised. This ensures that all outstanding tasks have been completed in the meantime and that a complete picture of the newly rehearsed workflow is available.

2.2.3 Phase 3: Overall Measurement of Effectiveness

Phase 3 serves to close the circle of effect at the level of the entire company and to review and sustainably ensure the effectiveness of improvement management as a whole. To achieve this, an overall analysis of the effectiveness of all implemented improvement projects is conducted. This comprehensive assessment is normally carried out once a year and compares the results achieved with the objectives set in the first phase.

In addition to the analysis of the effectiveness and the achievement of objectives, the recorded findings from the respective final reports of the individual improvement projects are compiled and evaluated. The resulting fields of action are again fed into the first phase as new topic proposals for improvements and included in the selection of topics for the next year.

The evaluation of all improvement projects processed and implemented in the last year shows the effect of these projects. This is crucial in order to assess the effectiveness of the company's handling of improvement projects. However, as only implemented improvements are assessed, this analysis does not provide an overall assessment of the quality of the work processes. The maturity model offers a holistic approach to assessing the maturity of organisations and work processes. It provides a detailed analysis of the state of each workflow under consideration. The maturity model is presented in detail in Sect. 4.2.

2.3 Limits of Improvement Management

The past successes achieved in a wide variety of companies from different sectors clearly speak for the continuous improvement of existing work processes. Although the reported results sound very tempting, the introduction of improvement management does not necessarily lead to success, and the improvement methods cannot necessarily be applied in every situation. Major obstacles and stumbling blocks to the successful implementation of these methods are in particular:

1. Lack of framework conditions
2. Lack of patience during the introduction
3. Time and costs
4. Fear of job loss among employees
5. More difficult to implement in the office area than in production

(1) Lack of framework conditions

For the successful continuous improvement of work processes, the necessary framework conditions must first be established and lived in the company. This often requires a rethinking and a targeted change of the existing corporate culture with a stronger involvement of all employees in the decision-making and change processes. The creation of these framework conditions is time-consuming and labour-intensive and must be based on a strong commitment from the entire management.

In many cases, improvement initiatives already fail because of the existing framework conditions in the company. Either the existing corporate culture does not provide support for the methods to improve work processes, or the will to anchor a corresponding corporate culture does not exist. Without the central framework conditions, however, no sustainable successes can be achieved with improvement management because the commitment of the management and the support of the employees are missing.

(2) Lack of patience during the introduction

Establishing successful improvement management takes a lot of time and patience. Before the actual improvement of work processes, the necessary foundations must first be laid. This includes the resolute establishment of the framework conditions, including the anchoring of the corresponding mindset in all of those involved. In addition, the know-how of both managers and employees must be built up. Only then can concrete improvement projects be tackled. All of this cannot be achieved within just a few months and requires a long-term commitment.

In addition, one must be aware that existing work processes cannot be optimised practically overnight. It is essential to work consistently on existing processes over a longer period of time in order to get them to the most efficient level possible. It is important to keep in mind that even work processes that appear to be optimal often have to be optimised again due to changes in the environment.

If a company finds itself in an acute economic and financial emergency, it requires quick and drastic measures to address the existing problems and to ensure its survival in the short term. In this case, the various methods of continuous improvement are much too slow and not effective enough. Here, business reengineering can perhaps offer an approach to find a solution.

(3) Time and costs

The optimisation of work processes requires a great deal of commitment from all staff involved as well as additional resources for the ongoing support in the implementation of the improvement topics to be worked on. This entails a temporal and financial expenditure that should not be underestimated. If the management is not willing to use these required resources in a targeted manner and to allocate the necessary financial means, the desired optimisations cannot be achieved. If employees are not given the freedom to support and advance the ongoing improvements in addition to their daily tasks, they will always prioritise the ongoing activities.

It is crucial that the ideas for improvement which provide a great benefit are already prioritised during the topic selection. It makes no sense to pour too many resources into minor or rarely used work processes.

(4) Fear of job loss among employees

In many companies, the optimisation of work processes is primarily understood as an approach to reduce the workload and thus to reduce costs. As a result, employees often do not support improvement management for fear of losing their jobs. In fact, they may even try to prevent improvement projects.

Only if it is possible to dispel the employees' fears and to guarantee that they will not lose their jobs as a result of improvement management can the support of all those involved be won.

(5) More difficult to implement in the office area than in production

Compared to production processes, office workflows are often less clearly defined and structured. Instead of standardised products that are manufactured in large quantities, a multitude of changing factors influence the output in the office sector. This leads to varying workflows that are more difficult to grasp and optimise. According to Brenner (2018), the main challenges in the office sector compared to production lie in the following aspects:

- *Transparency of processes:* Activities and results in the office area are often less visible and less transparent than in production. This makes it difficult to identify waste and potential for improvement.
- *More difficult standardisation:* The standardisation of work processes in the office sector is more difficult than in production. Activities are generally less repetitive and also vary greatly in their execution. This makes standardisation more difficult, which is, however, necessary as a prerequisite for optimising work processes.
- *Repeatability of the work steps:* In the office sector, activities vary much more than in production. This means that the repeatability of the work steps is lower and the processes are more irregular.
- *Measurability of processes:* The definition of operational key figures and their measurability in administrative work processes is much more demanding than for the corresponding processes in production.

In spite of these obstacles, the ongoing improvement of office workflows offers enormous potential for companies. If these critical points are addressed and dealt with consistently, nothing stands in the way of a successful implementation.

> **Recommended Reading** For more in-depth information on optimising office workflows, I recommend the book *Lean Administration—Verschwendung in Büros erkennen, analysieren, beseitigen* by Jörg Brenner (2018). In his book, the author describes how office processes can be made leaner based on the seven types of waste.

References

Brenner, J. (2018). *Lean administration: Verschwendung in Büros erkennen, analysieren, beseitigen*. München: Carl Hanser Verlag.

Ohno, T. (2019). *The Toyota production system*. Productivity Press.

Process Improvement Methods 3

Overview of Improvement Methods
Improvement management is not a recent movement, but is based on a long tradition. Numerous different methods which focus on optimally fulfilling customer needs with efficient and effective work processes exist. In this chapter, the most common methods are briefly introduced. It shows how they emerged, which basic principles are followed and how they are applied in practice.

Comparison of the Different Methods
The differences between the various methods and their characteristics are shown, and the advantages and disadvantages are compared.

Selection of the Most Suitable Method
Depending on the complexity of the issue, these methods can be used specifically to optimise work processes. Here it is illustrated when which method is most sensibly used.

M. Hofmann, *A Holistic Approach to Process Optimisation*, Management for Professionals, https://doi.org/10.1007/978-3-658-34097-1_3

3.1 Overview of Improvement Methods

As already indicated in Chap. 1, improvement management is not a new movement, but is based on a long tradition instead. Over time and depending on cultural circumstances, different methods have developed. They have strongly influenced each other and are partly based on the same principles and values. However, they set different priorities and sometimes differ greatly in their approach and implementation. Six Sigma, for example, relies on a distinct mathematical approach to record, measure and track irregularities. The Kaizen method, on the other hand, uses a strong visual component.

Depending on the problem and the existing basics, not all methods are equally suitable for dealing with the different improvement topics. For example, the mathematical approach of Six Sigma is difficult to apply to heterogeneous processes. In general, the following principle applies: the more complex the problem and the more employees and departments are involved in a workflow you hope to improve, the more comprehensive the planned improvement project should be approached.

The range of different improvement methods can be used accordingly to select the most optimal approach with the most suitable tools and aids depending on the problem. Figure 3.1 gives an overview of the most important improvement methods

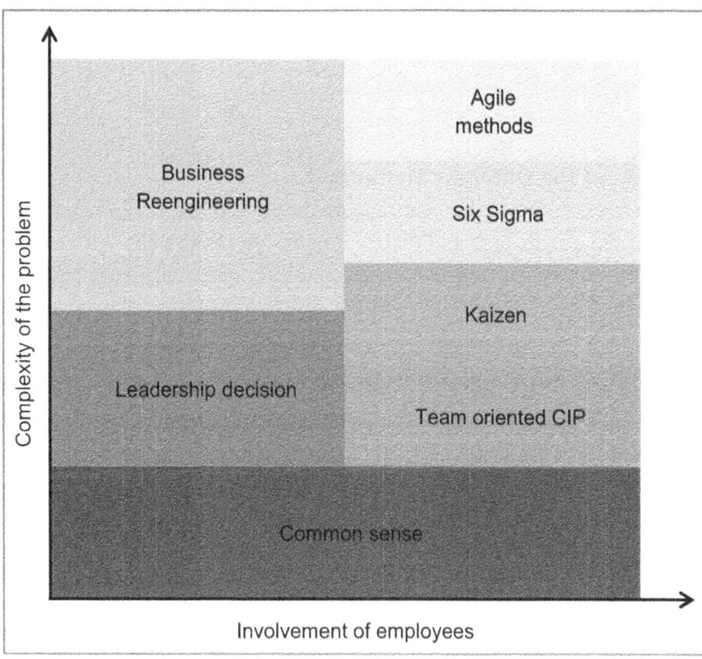

Fig. 3.1 Overview of improvement methods (based on Töpfer 2009)

and relates them to the complexity of the problem and the involvement of the employees concerned with their application.

Before launching an improvement project, it is important to weigh the benefits against the costs. It makes little sense to choose a costly and resource-intensive approach for a small, insignificant improvement. On the other hand, for more complex problems, more comprehensive methods are needed that help to cope with the complexity. It is often forgotten that simple problems can be solved very quickly and without elaborate methods, but with a portion of common sense. If only one team is affected, optimisation within the framework of the team-oriented continuous improvement process (CIP) is usually sufficient. Only more complex cross-team and cross-divisional issues justify the use of more elaborate methods such as Kaizen or Six Sigma.

Common Sense

Many improvements in work processes can be achieved without an elaborate improvement project. It is usually sufficient if the employees involved have a certain amount of leeway within clearly defined tasks, competences and responsibilities and can independently make simple adjustments to the existing work processes and the individual work steps. This is illustrated by the following example:

- Previously, the receptionist's task was to collect letters ready for dispatch from all departments in the designated outboxes every evening at 5:30 pm. This tour took about 10 min every day, with only 2–3 outboxes containing letters ready for dispatch. Since all staff members pass by the reception on their way home every evening anyway, the idea came up that everyone should deposit their mail there directly. After a short consultation with all those involved, it was decided to introduce this innovation immediately.

When implementing such simple measures, it is important that everyone involved is informed about them and that clear rules exist and are consistently lived by. In this case, for example, there is a rule that outgoing letters must be at reception by 5:30 pm. However, this also means that the mail must not be sent earlier.

Leadership Decision

In my everyday professional life, I am regularly confronted with cases in which a supervisor does not assume their actual responsibilities as a boss and, instead of making a clear leadership decision, they conduct elaborate improvement workshops with their team. The purpose of these workshops lies only in the aim to delegate the responsibility for the upcoming decision to the team. This happens, for example, when it is unclear who has to take on additional work steps, as the following example shows:

- As part of the commentary on the monthly financial statement, a detailed report on the development of the number of employees in all areas must now be prepared. This causes an hour of extra work and is very time-sensitive due to the tight deadlines. It is unclear who has to prepare this evaluation in the team. Therefore, the team leader organises a joint meeting to clarify how the process should be done in the future and who should do the work.

A clear leadership decision by the supervisor would have sufficed here. But since they did not want to make themselves unpopular with anyone, they preferred to let the team decide. To avoid such cases as much as possible, clearly defined responsibilities are needed. These determine who has to make which decision. In addition, a corresponding corporate culture is needed so that the responsibilities are lived out in everyday life and do not just exist on paper.

The Different Methods

After the discussion on common sense and management decisions, the following pages describe the most important improvement methods that have developed over the last hundred years. They follow a holistic approach and are used when dealing with more complex issues.

3.1.1 Team-Oriented Continuous Improvement Process (CIP)

Improving work processes often begins with small steps. Especially simple optimisations in everyday life are best implemented in well-rehearsed teams. In short joint workshops, a lot can be achieved this way. The continuous improvement process is an ideal framework for optimising team-internal processes. This is generally abbreviated to CIP. As a positive side effect of optimising work processes, team cohesion and cooperation are improved at the same time.

The CIP Method

For the CIP method, the underlying mindset is crucial. The method is based on the continuous optimisation of processes in small steps with the involvement of the employees concerned. The method is often equated with the Kaizen method, which was developed by Toyota in Japan. This is true insofar as both methods are based on the same fundamental attitude and have the employees play a central role in the optimisation of work processes. However, in my experience, companies that employ the CIP method tend to implement selective improvements based on an internal suggestion system. In contrast, the Kaizen method is more comprehensive and more systematic in its approach to cross-sectoral improvement throughout the company.

The CIP method is based on the process optimisation procedure as it is used in the Deming Circle, which was developed by William Edwards Deming (see description in Sect. 1.2). Here, an improvement is approached in four steps, whereby it is crucial that a feedback from the fourth step back to the first step takes place. Figure 3.2 shows the respective key question of the CIP method in connection with the Deming Circle.

Prerequisite

In order to be able to successfully apply and anchor the CIP method in a company, an overarching improvement culture must first be established. In addition, the

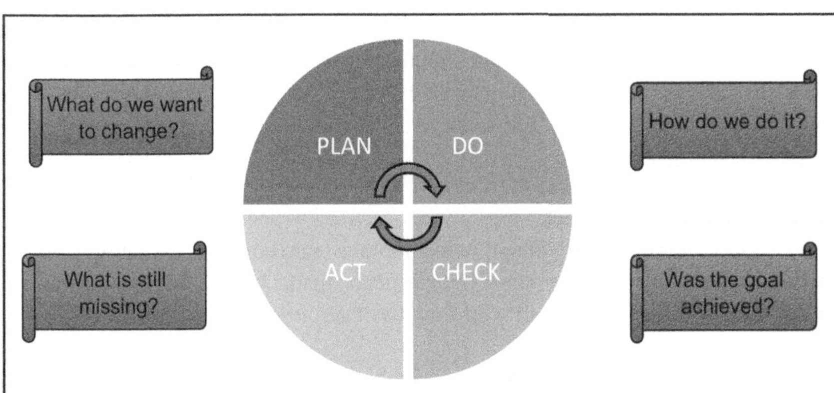

Fig. 3.2 Parallels between the Deming Circle and the team CIP (based on Deming 2018)

employees must know the method and be familiar with the procedure. Furthermore, it is helpful to introduce a functioning internal suggestion system, as this contributes a lot to the identification of potential improvement topics.

It is crucial for success that the suggestions for improvement developed in the team are implemented promptly. If they are implemented slowly or not at all, the motivation of the employees involved quickly decreases. In addition, the support of the management must be given in order to clarify points of contact with other teams.

Procedure

To support the introduction of the CIP method in a team, the essential framework conditions for successful implementation must be created beforehand. This includes reserving a time slot for a joint activity on a regular basis (e.g. once a month). Furthermore, possible improvement topics should be collected continuously via an internal suggestion system or a team-internal topic repository. The improvement workshop itself proceeds according to the following four steps:

Step 1: Choosing the Improvement Topic

If an improvement topic has not already been jointly selected before the workshop, this is done at the beginning of the meeting. The input from the internal suggestion system or the topics from the team's internal topic collection serve as a basis. Normally, the topic with the greatest benefit in the short term is chosen for processing.

Step 2: Analysis of the Problem Areas

The chosen topic is worked on together in the team. It is important that the problem areas are first precisely determined and analysed. It is advisable to observe the critical work steps directly at the respective workplace. Afterwards, optimisations for the individual problem areas are worked out together.

Step 3: Implement the Improvement

The solutions developed are directly implemented in the next step and built into the existing workflow. It is important that the adapted process is simulated immediately. This is the easiest way to determine whether the optimisations achieve the desired effect or whether further adjustments are necessary. Important: The adjustments must be documented and immediately incorporated into the existing work documents and instructions.

Step 4: Checking the Effect

A few weeks after the improvement workshop, the team conducts a joint review. The aim is to determine whether the improvements made have achieved the desired benefits and whether the overall workflow has been improved.

It is essential that the individual workshops do not become too extensive. They should take no more than half a workday. In addition, the solutions developed must be simple and able to be implemented rapidly.

During the workshop, one team member takes the lead to ensure the organisational framework. This includes facilitation, time management and documentation of decisions made. In my experience, it is beneficial for team building to give this role to another staff member on a rotating basis. It is also important that the team leader sees himself as part of the team and does not overrule the team's decisions.

Internal Suggestion Scheme

The internal suggestion system is a tool that aims to use the idea potential of all employees in a company. Employees can enter their suggestions for improvement by means of idea cards or, today, partly also via electronic tools. More and more often, the suggestions with the greatest benefit for the company are rewarded, and the initiator receives a bonus.

The internal suggestion scheme serves as a basis for internal improvements, and companies often use it in connection with the CIP method. However, it is not only used in conjunction with the CIP method, but it is also employed in other improvement methods such as Kaizen or Six Sigma.

3.1.2 Kaizen

Taiichi Ohno was employed as an engineer and production manager at Toyota in Japan after World War II. In order to master the many challenges after the war and to build up and advance production, he travelled to America several times to study Henry Ford's production system. As Henry Ford's system of mass production was not suitable for Toyota's production, which consisted of small quantities of different types of cars, he adapted it to Toyota's needs. This developed into the Toyota Production System and the Kaizen method. As Fig. 3.3 shows, Kai in Japanese means change/transformation and Zen means for the better.

Kaizen is both a methodical concept and a holistic philosophy, according to which a step-by-step optimisation of a product or a work process is aimed for. The improvement is tackled in workshops, together with the employees concerned. These employees are then also at the centre of the Kaizen method. The focus is on aligning all activities to the needs of the customer and eliminating any kind of waste in the work processes.

This does not only pertain to actual waste (muda) and the seven types of waste (see the description of the types of waste in Sect. 1.3.2). Rather, it is also about avoiding inequality (mura) and overburdening (muri). According to Ohno (2019), only the elimination of these 3Ms leads to efficient and error-free work processes. Figure 3.4 describes the meaning of these 3Ms.

An essential goal of the Kaizen method is higher customer satisfaction, since customer acquisition is more expensive than customer retention. To ensure customer satisfaction, the factors 'cost reduction', 'quality assurance' and 'speed' are foregrounded.

The prerequisite for the continuous development of work processes with the Kaizen method is a lived cooperative corporate culture and the standardisation of processes. Building on this, the four basic principles 'flow principle', 'tact principle', 'pull principle' and 'zero error principle' are applied. These are described in Fig. 3.5.

Just-in-time management has developed from these basic principles of Toyota's production model. The goal here is to have the right parts available in the right quantity at the right time in the right place. This reduces intermediate and final storage and eliminates waste.

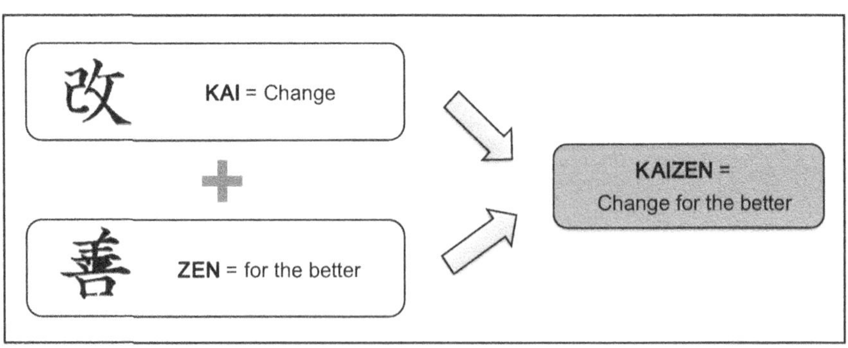

Fig. 3.3 Meaning of Kaizen (based on Ohno 2019)

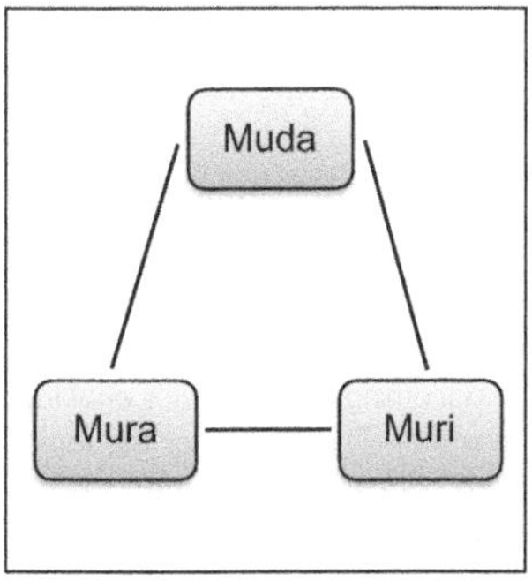

Muda: (Waste) Muda is the term for waste. This must be avoided throughout the entire process of creating a product or service.

Mura: (Inequality) Mura is the term for the disparity between the use of resources and the result or between man and machine. This inequality must be eliminated.

Muri: (Overburdening) Muri is the term for overburdening people or equipment Overburdening people results in safety, health and quality problems. Overburdening equipment causes breakdowns and defects.

Fig. 3.4 Importance of the 3Ms (based on Ohno 2019)

Flow principle

The flow principle promotes fast and continuous material and information flows. Intermediate storage between the work steps should be eliminated. This prevents work that has been started from being left undone.

Example: Instead of collecting customer enquiries in the sales office and transmitting them to the back office once a day, they are passed on continuously.

Tact principle

The Tact principle involves the even distribution of work content to the individual workstations. This helps to balance out existing capacity fluctuations and to increase efficiency.

The application of the tact principle brings an increase in efficiency, especially in production, as it can smooth out the different workloads of the various production stations.

Pull principle

Comparable to a supermarket shelf, with the pull principle the customer's demand controls the replenishment and thus the workflow. Only what is in demand is produced.

This means that sales are recorded promptly and that replenishment can take place quickly and efficiently.

Example: Brochures are only reprinted when the minimum stock in the delivery is not reached.

Zero-error principle

The question of the cause of the error must be more important than the question of who caused it. If an error is detected, the concern is to look for causes and find solutions so that this error does not happen again.

To minimise the number of mistakes, the following points are important:

- Don't make mistakes!
- Do not pass on mistakes!
- Do not accept mistakes!

Fig. 3.5 Basic principles of Kaizen (based on Ohno 2019)

A decisive success factor of the Kaizen method is based on the inclusion of upstream and downstream partner companies in the consideration of overarching process flows. Optimisation thus focuses not only on the work processes of the company's own operations but also on the work processes of suppliers and customers as well as the common interfaces between the companies involved. Only this close networking and optimal coordination enables the use of just-in-time management without the risk of delivery bottlenecks.

The Workshop

Improvement projects according to the Kaizen method are usually worked on and implemented in workshops. These workshops take place under the leadership of a trained Kaizen coach and with the employees involved.

The Kaizen topics are dealt with according to the procedure shown in Fig. 3.6.

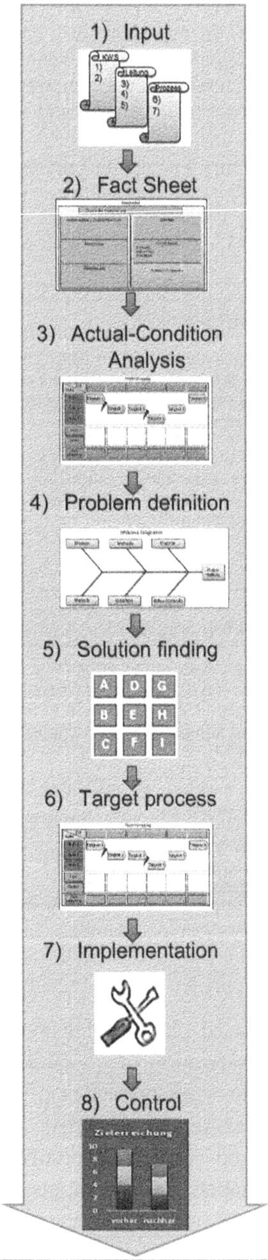

A comprehensive planning of the upcoming Kaizen topics enables an efficient and targeted improvement. The inputs for the topic identification are derived from the company goals, the process reviews and the feedback from the employees.

For each Kaizen workshop, a Fact Sheet is first created with the following contents: Initial situation, delimitation, goals, participants and timeframe for implementation. It is essential to develop this Fact Sheet together with the sponsor.

The basis for optimising the workflow is the current situation. Based on the existing process documentation, the situation is recorded and documented together with the employees concerned in the form of a Process Mapping.

In the jointly developed Process Mapping, the problems of the workflow are drawn in. A detailed description is created for each problem. It is essential that no solution is described yet; only the problem is recorded for the time being .

In the next step, the individual problems are analysed indetail and possible solutions for optimisations are developed. Depending on the number and complexity of the problems , prioritisation and focusing is recommended.

The solutions developed are incorporated into a newly designed target process in the form of a Process Mapping. This target process is then simulated and reviewed together with the workshop participants.

To each measure decided on in the workshop, a person responsible is assigned. This person ensures that the adjustments are completed by the agreed deadline. For a sustainable optimisation, the adaptation of the existing documentation is also crucial.

The effectiveness of the measures taken is checked and measured with a review a few weeks after the workshop At the same time, it is considered whether further measures are necessary for an optimal workflow.

Fig. 3.6 Kaizen process

The Roles in Kaizen

Kaizen is a comprehensive philosophy that influences not only the work processes but also the working methods and behaviour of all employees. In its implementation, continuous improvement is pursued in small steps. Kaizen is a part of the daily management and involves all employees.

The roles in Kaizen are distributed as follows:

- *Management:* Responsible for anchoring Kaizen in the strategy and ensuring the necessary framework for implementation. The management sets the overarching goals and ensures that they are met.
- *Cadres:* Act as sponsors of Kaizen issues. They support the processing and implementation of complex improvement projects. They also help to remove obstacles.
- *Direct supervisors:* Encourage and promote the improvement culture in the company by setting clear goals. They support the implementation, recognise optimisations and give active feedback to the employees.
- *Kaizen coach:* Takes over the implementation of Kaizen issues by ensuring coordination with the sponsor, leading the workshops with the employees concerned as well as ensuring the implementation of the measures decided upon.
- *Improvement community:* Acts as an enabler and culture promoter for cadres and employees. This includes communication, support for questions concerning the method and tools and training.
- *Employees:* Actively help in the processing and implementation of Kaizen issues. Thus, they become enablers and culture promoters themselves.

Five Steps to Efficient Organisation

The five steps to efficient organisation are known as 5S in the Kaizen method. They pursue the efficient design of workplaces and form the basis for the application of Kaizen. The 5S are explained in Fig. 3.7.

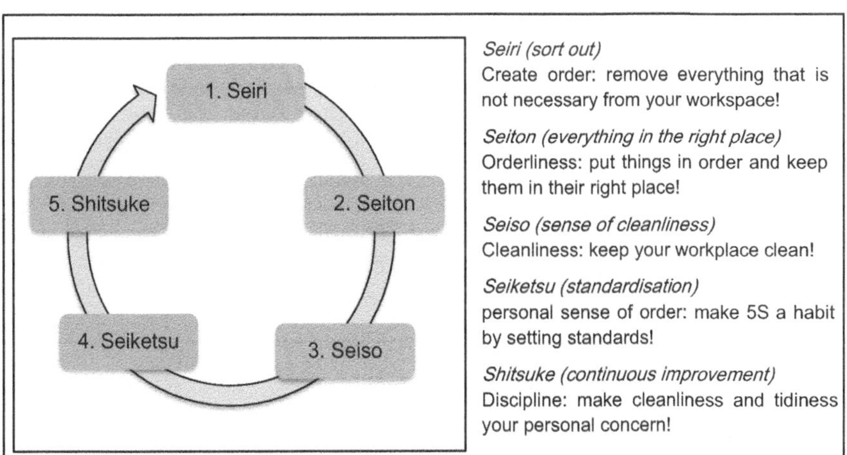

Fig. 3.7 5S—5 steps to an efficient organisation (based on Ohno 2019)

3.1.3 Six Sigma

Six Sigma is an improvement method developed in the USA in the 1990s by Bill Smith, an engineer and scientist at Motorola. The existing methods at that time (such as Kaizen) were not concrete and measurable enough for Bill Smith. Therefore, in developing the Six Sigma method, he relied on a distinct mathematical approach to assess the performance of work processes and their outputs. The aim of the method is to reduce recurring errors in work processes by the means of a structured approach and the corresponding methodological tools. A key feature is the measurability of process outputs using statistical tools.

The processing and implementation of improvement projects, which are approached according to the Six Sigma method, takes place within the framework of an improvement project involving the employees concerned. This project is carried out in five phases according to the DMAIC approach described in Fig. 3.8.

Ideas for improvement projects according to the Six Sigma method can be generated from various sources. One important input is the mathematical measurements of process performance and key figures. However, it is important to include all sources for comprehensive thematic coverage. Figure 3.9 shows the most important sources.

Figure 3.10 shows the procedure for processing and implementing improvement projects according to the DMAIC method and describes the content of the individual project phases.

The optimal number of employees in project teams to work on and implement a Six Sigma project depends strongly on the complexity of the improvement project and the number of employees involved in the workflow to be optimised. Ideally, the team should consist of four to eight participants. If the team is too small, it is difficult to cover all essential aspects. If the team is too large, cooperation becomes cumbersome, and the amount of work increases significantly.

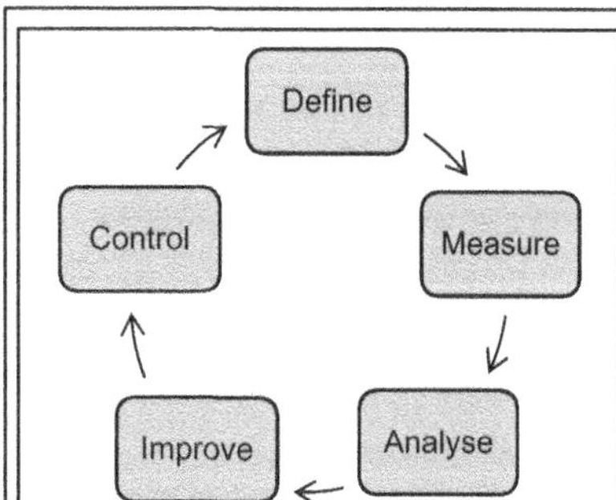

The abbreviation DMAIC stands for the following terms: Define, Measure, Analyse, Improve and Control. They stand for the continuous improvement of existing work processes.

For the development of new work processes that do not yet exist, the DMAIC model was extended to the DMADV model. The last two letters stand for Design and Verify.

Fig. 3.8 Six Sigma—DMAIC (based on Lunau 2014)

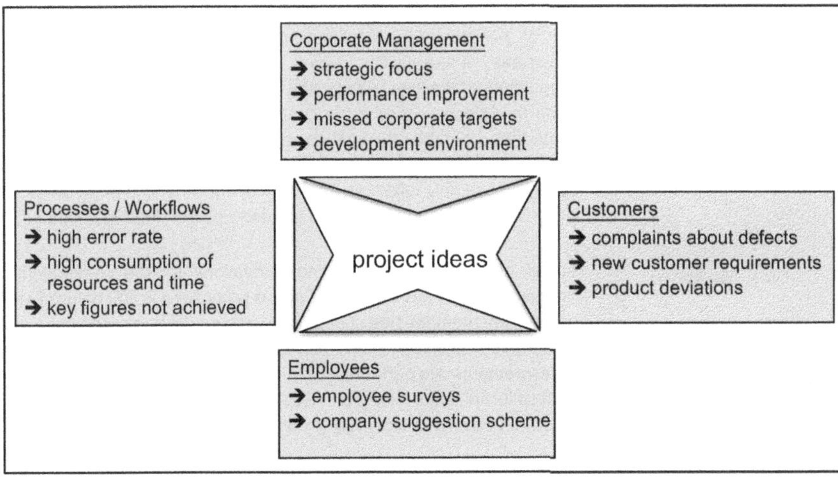

Fig. 3.9 Origin of project ideas in Six Sigma

The processing and implementation of the improvement project takes place in several short workshops, which extend over several weeks. However, the entire processing time until the completion of the project should take no more than 2 to 3 months at the most.

The Roles in Six Sigma

In Six Sigma, different expert levels can be reached. These depend on the professional experience gained as well as additional training courses completed. The levels are structured as follows:

- *Yellow Belt:* first experiences with Six Sigma
- *Green Belt:* able to manage projects independently
- *Black Belt:* able to manage complex projects
- *Master Black Belt:* able to lead improvement organisations

All these certified expert levels can be found in different functions of the companies. They play a decisive role in the processing and implementation of Six Sigma projects. The following roles are distinguished:

- *Corporate management:* It is responsible for anchoring the Six Sigma method in the corporate strategy and ensures the necessary framework conditions for the processing and implementation of the individual Six Sigma projects. It triggers the Six Sigma initiatives and monitors their implementation.
- *Champion:* The Champion steers the Six Sigma initiatives in the company by evaluating potential improvement projects and proposing them for implementation. They appoint the project leaders and support them in the processing and

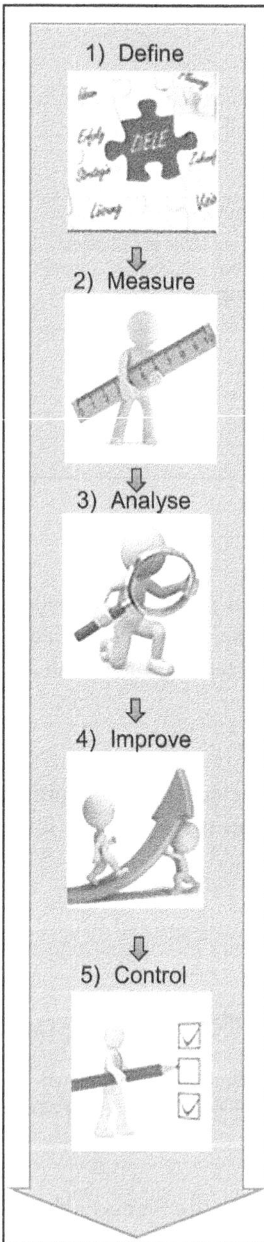

Out of the previously identified project ideas for optimising work processes, a specific Six Sigma project is nominated. This is formulated as precisely as possible in the project charter. The focus is on the question of who the customers are, what they want and what they demand. In addition, the project goals, the expected project benefits and the project boundaries are formulated in detail. In this phase, the following tools are used, among others: SIPOC, VOC-CTQ-Analysis (These tools are described in detail in chapter 4).

In the measurement phase, the foundations for the subsequent problem analysis are collected. For this purpose, it is first determined which measurement data contribute to a more precise assessment of the problem and how these can be obtained. Then the specified measurements are performed and the results are compiled in the data collection plan. Based on these process measurements, the real problem becomes a statistical problem.

In the analysis phase, a detailed process and data analysis is first carried out based on the collected measurement data. This includes, among other things, the analysis of the process times, the recording of time wasters and the determination of error sources. Subsequently, the causes of deviations and irregularities are identified and described. The most important tools in this phase are: Process -Flow Diagram (Process Mapping), Ishikawa Diagram, Spaghetti Diagram and Pareto Chart (These tools are described in detail in chapter 4).

After the detailed survey, evaluation and analysis of the individual fields of action, optimisation and harmonisation ideas are developed together with the employees concerned, measures are evaluated and their implementation is planned. This is always executed using a number-oriented approach. This means that the expected impact of the optimisation approaches is substantiated with concrete measurements and targets. Important tools in this phase are the Cost-Benefit Analysisand the Implementation Plan (These tools are described in detail in chapter 4).

Finally, it is verified whether the defined measures have been implemented successfully and whether the desired effect has been achieved. In addition, a suitable control instrument for the future monitoring of the process is established and passed on to the process owner. This control instrument contains clearly defined process indicators and performance values, which are to be recorded and reviewed by the process owner with regular statistical measurements.

Fig. 3.10 Six Sigma process

subsequent implementation. In addition, they are present at the start and completion of the project. This role is usually performed by a Master Black Belt.
- *Direct supervisors:* Support the improvement culture and the Six Sigma initiative in the company by communicating the method and the successes achieved to their employees. They also provide the resources for the improvement projects and support cross-departmental discussions.
- *Project leaders:* The project leaders manage the Six Sigma improvement projects and ensure their implementation in daily operations. For this purpose, they lead the project workshops with the employees involved and are responsible for the project documentation. They impart methodological competence and knowledge of the tools used to the employees concerned. Depending on the complexity of the issue, the role of the project leader is taken on by a Black Belt or a Green Belt.
- *Employees:* Work on the improvement projects and contribute their experience from day-to-day business and their expertise. They implement the developed improvement measures and ensure their correct application in everyday life. Ideally, all key employees have Yellow Belt training and corresponding Six Sigma experience.
- *Other supporters:* Contribute their experience and expertise and participate selectively in the different phases of the project. These may be, for example, the following groups:
  - External Six Sigma experts
  - Suppliers
  - Customers
  - Partner companies

The Mathematical Component of Six Sigma

The Six Sigma method relies heavily on statistically measurable data for both process improvement and the control of ongoing processes. As a result, even small changes can be demonstrated quickly and precisely, and appropriate corrective measures can be initiated and implemented in a timely manner.

Evaluation by means of statistics requires standardised work processes with a high number of repetitions. This is often difficult, especially in administration. Therefore, the mathematical component of Six Sigma is primarily used by industrial companies in manufacturing. Figure 3.11 describes the normal distribution curve, which according to Knecht and Bertschi (2013) is the most frequently used type of probability distribution in practice and thus plays a central role in Six Sigma.

In addition to the standard deviation, there are a large number of other statistical parameters that are used in the context of Six Sigma. An example of concrete application and calculation of key figures can be found in Lunau (2014). A selection of the most important indicators is listed here:

- *DPU (Defects per Unit):* Measures the number of defects per unit. Since all possible defects are measured, multiple defects per unit are also possible.

In the term Six Sigma, sigma (σ) stands for the standard deviation of a measurand. The standard deviation is a measure of the statistical dispersion of the measurand around its mean value and is used in connection with the normal distribution.

For a normally distributed measurand (many measurands found in practice are at least approximately normally distributed), 99.73% of all measured values have a deviation of no more than 3 sigma from the mean.

Six sigma stands for "six standard deviations". Thus 99.9999998% of all measurements are within the target value. In practice, the mean value shifts by 1.5 sigma over time. Thus, a quality of 99.9997% is achieved. This corresponds to 3.4 errors in one million error possibilities. The figure opposite shows the curve with a normal distribution.

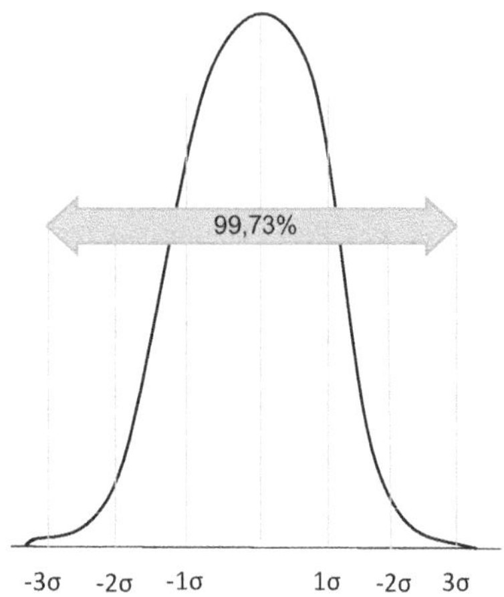

Fig. 3.11 The normal distribution curve (based on Knecht and Bertschi 2013)

- *PPM (Parts per Million):* Measures how many units out of one million are defective. Used for tracking defect occurrence during the implementation of the improvement project and for sustainable quality measurement and external benchmarks.
- *OEE (Overall Equipment Efficiency):* Measures the performance of production equipment by determining the utilisation of equipment in relation to availability.
- *Correlation analysis:* Measures the linear relationship between two variables and shows what proportion of the dispersion can be explained by the dependence of the two variables.

The mathematical component is also reflected in various tools used in Six Sigma projects. One example is the Pareto chart, which is described in Sect. 4.1.9.

3.1.4 Business Reengineering

The term business reengineering was coined in the USA in the 1990s. In contrast to the methods of continuous improvement of work processes such as Kaizen or Six Sigma, it is not about optimising existing work processes. The focus of business reengineering is on radically redesigning the essential processes including the grown organisation. Business reengineering concerns the question of how the work to be done can be organised most efficiently in view of today's market requirements and the latest technological possibilities.

Implementing improvements in small cautious steps is not possible from a business reengineering perspective. It is all or nothing. Michael Hammer and James Champy, the developers of the method, define it as follows: 'Business reengineering is, strictly speaking, a fundamental rethinking and radical redesign of companies or essential company processes. The result is improvements by several orders of magnitude in critical, nowadays important and measurable performance variables in the areas of cost, quality, service and time' (Hammer and Champy 1993).

According to Hammer and Champy (1993), the dynamic environment with rapidly changing competitive forces influences the existing business world and its environment to such an extent that organisations that were created for a specific business field can no longer be optimised in such a way that they can continue to exist in the new environment. Figure 3.12 shows the competitive forces acting on the company's business model.

The most important advantage of business reengineering compared to conventional improvement methods is that no consideration has to be given to existing and historically grown work processes and entrenched structures. Aligned with the company's goals, optimal processes are newly developed and introduced top-down. This is much faster and brings about more radical changes than ongoing development with the involvement of the employees concerned.

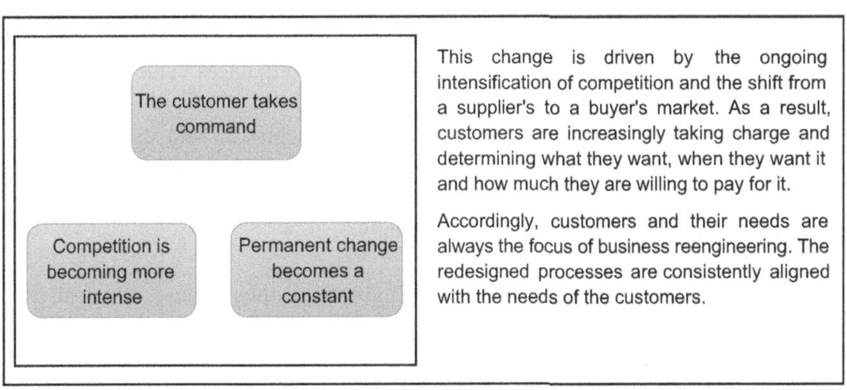

Fig. 3.12 Changing competitive forces (based on Hammer and Champy 1993)

On the other hand, this uncompromising approach also harbours significant dangers. With the resolute redesign of workflows, functioning and well-established processes are thrown overboard. Valuable know-how is lost as a result. In addition, it takes some time until the new top-down work processes are in place and function smoothly. In the transition phase, this can lead to higher inefficiencies and greater waste in the process, as well as increased quality problems. In addition, there is a risk that staff will not back the new processes and will be reluctant to accept and support the introduction.

Solution Approaches in Business Reengineering

Depending on the current starting situation and the target state of the process to be redefined, there are different approaches in business reengineering according to Fig. 3.13.

These multi-layered approaches and their profound effects on the central work processes, the employees, the management and the corporate culture show that business reengineering is far more than just a method for making work processes more efficient. Rather, business reengineering is a holistic management approach that radically changes the entire company very quickly. The four essential elements of this change, which influence each other, are, according to Hammer and Champy (1993):

- *The business processes:* This is the central point of change with business reengineering. It includes the way in which the daily activities are done. The determination of the processes has a corresponding effect on the composition of the teams and departments and thus influences the organisational structure.
- *The organisational structure and associated jobs:* Business reengineering increasingly relies on integrated processes. In order to be able to optimally carry out the resulting activities, multidimensional job profiles are increasingly being developed, and process teams are being employed. These new job profiles and organisational forms in turn influence the management and evaluation systems of companies.
- *The management and evaluation systems:* They ensure the recruitment, empowerment, evaluation and remuneration of the required staff and process teams. The assessment and evaluation of performance in turn influences value concepts and beliefs.
- *The value concepts and beliefs:* They include the issues and concerns that a company's employees believe are important and which they act upon. These value concepts and beliefs, in turn, must align with the requirements in the processes in order to execute them optimally.

Changes in the context of business reengineering thus always affect all four elements and change the company in the long term.

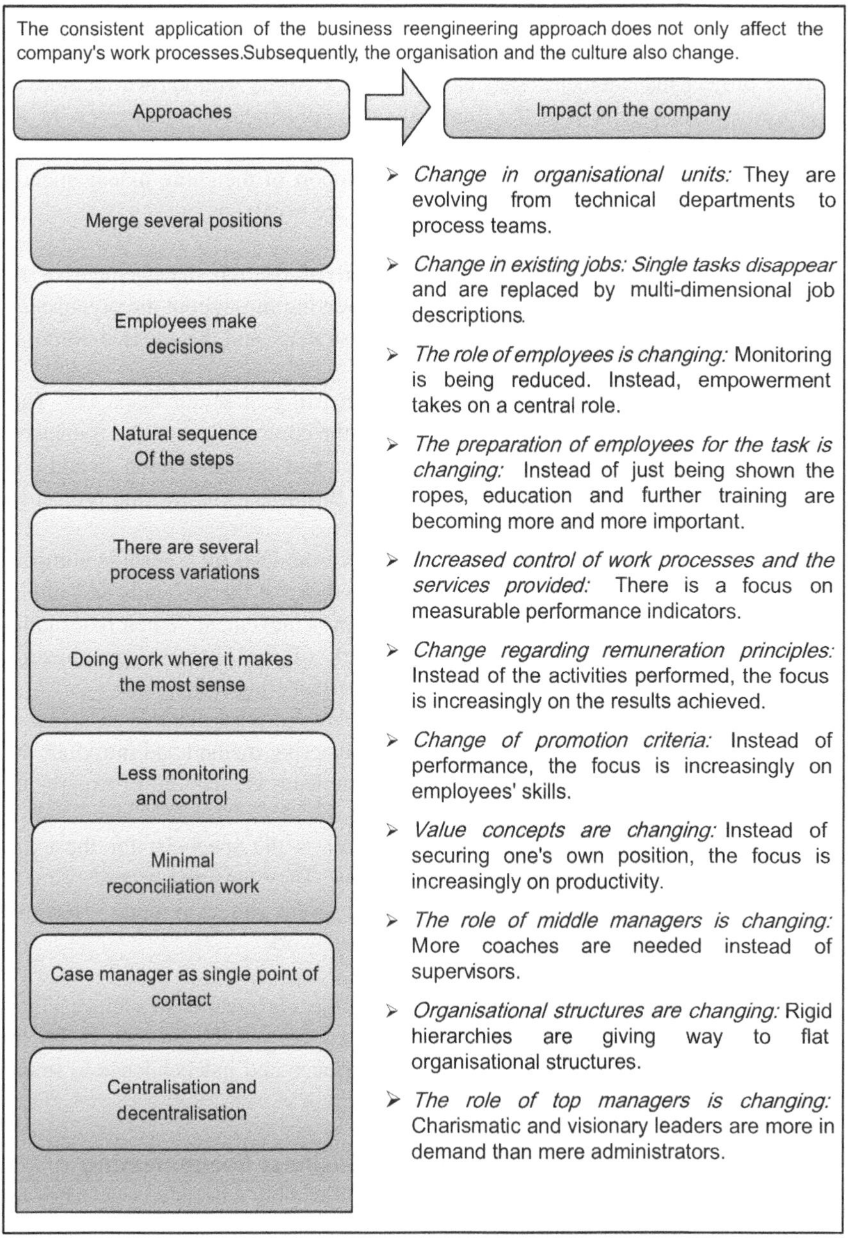

Fig. 3.13 Solution approaches in business reengineering (based on Hammer and Champy 1993)

The Roles in Business Reengineering

The essential roles of business reengineering are heavily based on the traditional roles of project management. The main difference to the well-known methods of improvement management is the much lower involvement of employees, as the redesign of processes is primarily top-down. However, identical to the other methods is that in business reengineering too, the full support of the entire management is crucial for success. In detail, the following roles are involved:

- *Leader:* This is a person who must be part of the top management of the company. The leader pushes business reengineering throughout the organisation and ensures the link to the overall corporate strategy and the adopted corporate goals.
- *Steering committee:* This is a committee consisting of senior managers. They define the business reengineering strategy for the company within the framework of the overall strategy and ensure its compliance and implementation. In addition, fundamental decisions regarding the ongoing business reengineering project are made and enforced in this committee.
- *Process owners:* The process owners each take the lead for a specific company process. They are responsible for the achievement of the set goals and initiate appropriate corrective measures in case of non-achievement. When redesigning their business process within the framework of the business reengineering method, they are part of the implementing reengineering team.
- *Reengineering team:* This is a group of people who push planned redesigns of processes with the help of the business reengineering method and introduce and anchor the newly defined work processes. The team is made up of experts and experienced employees.
- *Reengineering Czar:* The Reengineering Czar is the specialist for the entire business reengineering project in the company. They have the necessary methodological competence and manage the various tools and instruments. They also support the various reengineering teams in their work.

Since the launch of a business reengineering project is intended to achieve a rapid and radical change, additional external specialists are usually brought in for the implementation. These have the necessary experience and independence to implement such complex projects.

The Roles of Information Technology in Business Reengineering

In business reengineering, technological possibilities play a decisive role. They are used specifically for the following situations:

- The redesign of work processes is based on the latest developments in information technology. This is done with the aim of achieving the greatest possible efficiency.

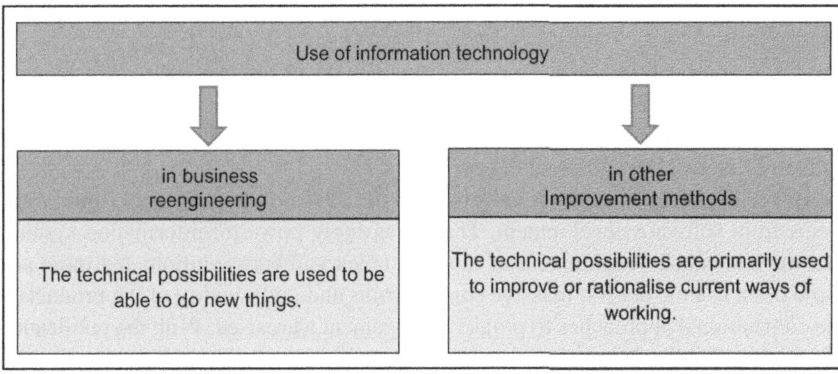

Fig. 3.14 Use of information technology (based on Hammer and Champy 1993)

– The management of the business reengineering project, including the implementation of the solution approaches decided upon, is carried out with strong support from information technology.

Due to the central role that IT systems play in business reengineering projects, it is particularly important to use information technology correctly. If it is used incorrectly, a redesign of efficient business processes can be severely hampered. Figure 3.14 shows the use of information technology in business reengineering in contrast to other improvement methods.

Risks of Business Reengineering

Due to the radical approach and the resulting major changes, business reengineering entails great uncertainties. Accordingly, the method is not easy to implement and carries a high risk. Therefore, the redesign of processes in business reengineering is primarily limited to core processes with great strategic importance that are worthy of improvement.

Business reengineering is often used by companies that are in a critical situation and need rapid and radical change. Such critical situations can be, for example, financial difficulties or major changes in the business environment, such as market changes due to new technologies or the market entry of a new competitor. In crisis situations, business reengineering is often the only solution to break up entrenched structures and inefficient business processes.

3.1.5 Agile Methods

The agile approach is not an improvement method in the true sense, but rather a holistic management philosophy. The focus is on the customer wishes, which are to be fulfilled quickly and in high quality with the help of a flat, dynamic organisation and short internal decision-making paths.

The origin of agile methods goes back to the 1990s of the twentieth century and stems from software development. The increasingly powerful information systems and the associated development of more complex software solutions led more and more often to time delays, massive cost overruns and poor quality of the products if the conventional approaches to project management were used. With the publication of the 'Agile Manifesto', a group of young developers wanted to counter these problems and revolutionise software development. In contrast to other management concepts, which were often developed by well-known consultancies and are protected by copyright, the 'Agile Manifesto' is available on the Internet under the link 'http://agilemanifeste.org' (Agilemanifeste.org 2001), freely accessible to all. The agile approach is based on the 12 principles shown in Fig. 3.15.

Initially, the focus of the agile approach was on agile collaboration and was used for the efficient management and execution of software development projects.

1) Our highest priority is to satisfy the customer through early and continuous delivery of valuable software.
2) Welcome changing requirements, even late indevelopment. Agile processes harness change for the customer's competitive advantage.
3) Deliver working software frequently, from a couple of weeks to a couple of months, with a preference to the shorter timescale.
4) Business people and developers must work together daily throughout the project.
5) Build projects around motivated individuals. Give them the environment and support they need, and trust them to get the job done.
6) The most efficient and effective method of conveying information to and within a development team is face-to-face conversation.
7) Working software is the primary measure of progress
8) Agile processes promote sustainable development. The sponsors, developers, and users should be able to maintain a constant pace indefinitely.
9) Continuous attention to technical excellence and good design enhances agility.
10) Simplicity - the art of maximizing the amountof work not done - is essential.
11) The best architectures, requirements, and designs emerge from self-organizing teams.
12) At regular intervals, the team reflects on how to become more effective, then tunes and adjusts its behaviour accordingly.

Fig. 3.15 The 12 principles of the Agile Manifesto (Source: agilemanifeste.org) (Agilemanifeste.org 2001)

Thanks to this approach, the development of complex and multi-layered products could be divided into manageable releases that build on each other. These releases are adapted or approved by the customer before and after implementation. This way, it is possible to respond flexibly to new or changing customer requirements at any time in order to increase overall customer satisfaction. At the same time, the handling of projects can be made more efficient, thanks to the reduction of bureaucracy and greater consideration of the human aspect.

Agile Management

Following the successes in software development, the approaches of the 'Agile Manifesto' are now used not only in project management but increasingly also as a management principle throughout the company. In addition, the importance of agile management continues to grow strongly due to the new challenges in connection with digitalisation. Companies that align their management philosophy with the agile approach differ from conventional companies in the following points:

- *Customer focus:* All activities of the company are strongly oriented towards the customer. Only things that bring added value to the customer are done. All other activities are eliminated as far as possible.
- *Organisation:* Compared to traditional companies, the organisation contains fewer intermediate levels and is therefore much flatter. This leads to shorter and more direct decision-making and communication channels.
- *Self-organisation:* Teams take over the organisation of their activities and organise the required outputs independently. This makes it possible to react more quickly to changing conditions and new customer needs.
- *Flexible structures:* Fixed team structures hardly exist anymore. Teams with the required skills and experience are put together anew depending on the task at hand.
- *Short distances to the customer:* The paths to the customer are kept as short as possible. This applies both to the contract for products and services and to rapid and regular customer feedback.
- *Communication:* Communication within the company is direct and open. In addition, employees are involved in decision-making at an early stage.

According to Roock and Wolf (2016), the term 'agility' can be defined as follows: autonomous teams with a business focus that take ownership of and responsibility for their process. Figure 3.16 shows the agile problem-solving approach compared to the classic solution approach.

The Scrum Method

Various independent methods subsequently emerged from the agile approach. The best-known one is Scrum, which is used to handle complex projects, primarily in software development. The name Scrum stems from the free kick situation in rugby. A project that is handled according to the Scrum method differs significantly from a conventional project. Self-organising teams play an essential role in the

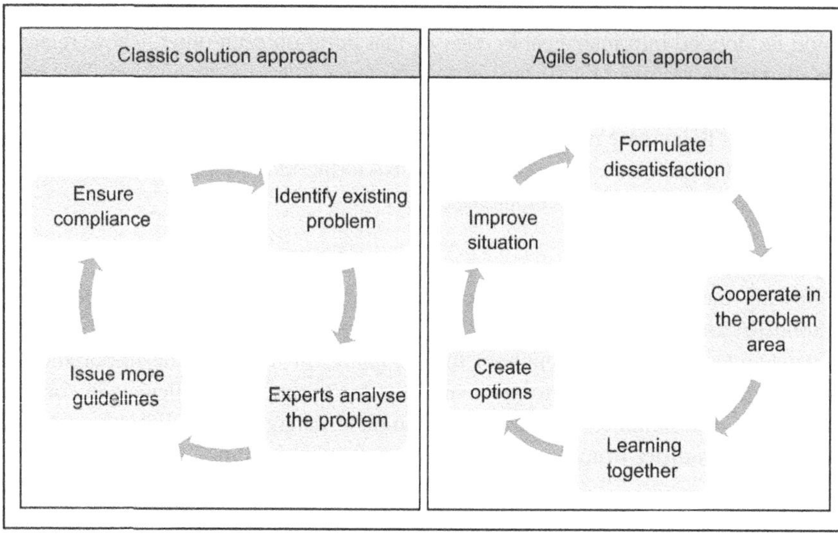

Fig. 3.16 Problem-solving approach in comparison (based on Roock and Wolf 2016)

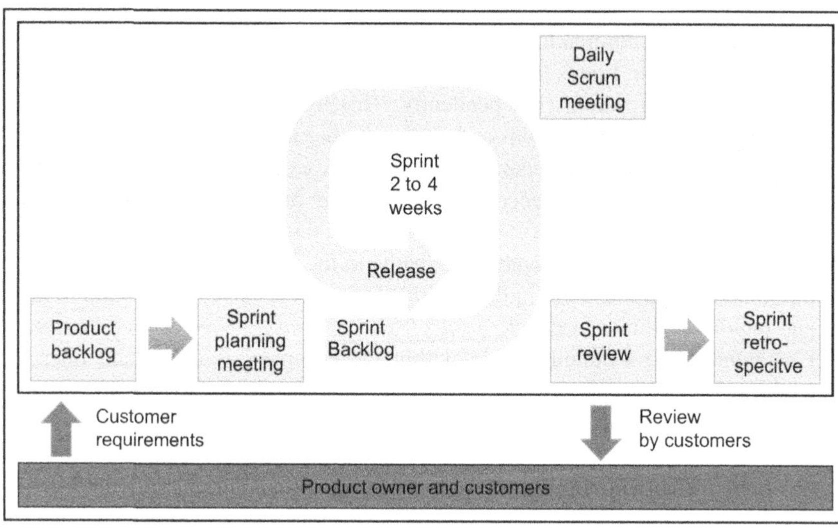

Fig. 3.17 Project process according to Scrum (based on Roock and Wolf 2016)

implementation of projects. Figure 3.17 shows the process of a project that is carried out according to the Scrum method: The Scrum team is at the centre of this process, working through the individual work packages in so-called sprints.

The individual steps of a project process according to Scrum are briefly explained below. The starting point is a product idea or a customer requirement.

- *Product backlog:* The product backlog is the basis for controlling the workload. This is where upcoming work packages (in Scrum these are called stories) are collected and managed by the product owner. It is crucial that the individual work packages can be developed and tested separately. It is essential that there is regular coordination with the customer regarding the prioritisation of outstanding work packages.
- *Sprint planning meeting:* In this meeting with the product owner and the executive team, it is determined which work packages from the product backlog are to be processed in the next sprint. These are transferred to the sprint backlog. The selection is based on the prioritisation of the individual work packages by the customer.
- *Sprint:* The sprint is the phase in which the previously agreed-on work packages are processed by the Scrum team. The sprint has a fixed duration, i.e. 2 weeks. During this time, the Scrum team must not be disturbed. At the end of the sprint, the Scrum team delivers the completed work packages.
- *Daily Scrum meeting:* In this meeting, the Scrum team reports on the progress made and agrees on the work to be done. Various visual tools are used to support the recording of the work progress and the outstanding activities. An example of this is the 'burn down chart, which is described in Sect. 4.1.13.
- *Sprint review:* This review takes place at the end of each sprint. Here, the Scrum team presents the created work package to the product owner and the customer as realistically as possible. The meeting serves to assess the work status and to provide feedback to the Scrum team.
- *Sprint retrospective:* The sprint retrospective concludes a sprint. It is an internal team review of the last sprint and helps to improve further cooperation within the Scrum team.
- *Acceptance of work packages:* Crucial to the success of agile projects is the rapid review of the completed work packages. This is first done internally at the end of each sprint by the responsible Scrum team and then by the final approval of the customer. This ongoing review enables rapid feedback to the product owner and adjustments to the product backlog.

Roles in Scrum

In Scrum projects, the following roles are of central importance:

- *The client:* The focus is on the client. The more precisely they can define their needs and requirements, the more accurately these can be realised by the team.
- *Product owner:* The product owner represents the interests of the customer and is responsible for the success of the product to be developed. Together with the customer, they define the product characteristics and prioritise the product backlog. They are also responsible for the acceptance of the completed work packages together with the customer.
- *The Scrum team:* The work packages are processed in the sprints by the Scrum team. The team answers to the customer for the entire development of the project, from the original idea to the delivered software. To achieve this, the Scrum team

is composed cross-functionally and organises itself. No fixed roles are defined within the team. These Scrum teams are put together specifically for each project. This means that the employees no longer work in fixed teams, but change Scrum teams depending on the upcoming projects.
- *Scrum master:* The expert team does not have a boss in the traditional sense. The Scrum master takes on the role of team coach, who ensures that the Scrum team can work effectively and efficiently.

Difference to Conventional Projects

Thanks to the rapid testing and acceptance of the individual work packages in agile projects, the implementation team receives immediate feedback from the client, and deficiencies can be identified at an early stage and rectified by the implementation team.

In conventionally managed projects, the acceptance of partial products is often missing. As a result, defects are often only detected at the end of the project or even during operation. This leads to higher costs due to troubleshooting, delays in the introduction and higher susceptibility to errors in the introduction phase.

The main benefits of projects carried out according to an agile approach are shorter time to market, higher quality, greater efficiency, more innovation and higher employee and customer satisfaction.

Parallels to the Improvement Methods

As with classic improvement methods such as Kaizen or Six Sigma, in agile methods, the employees concerned are also heavily involved in the optimisation process. Therefore, communication and mutual exchange between all those involved is of central importance.

Another parallel is the customer focus. The agile methods also focus on the customer and the activities are geared to their needs. In addition, in the Scrum method, the customer is directly involved in the process when prioritising the individual work packages and accepting the completed sub-products.

3.2 Comparison of the Different Methods

The methods for optimising work processes considered in the book have emerged over the last 150 years. Their developers were partly inspired by existing approaches. The two American pioneers Frederick Winslow Taylor and Henry Ford are considered to be the origin of today's process and improvement management. With the development and successful introduction of industrial manufacturing in the automobile industry, they laid the foundation for the improvement methods that exist today. It is therefore not surprising that the various improvement methods show strong parallels. Nevertheless, there are sometimes major and essential differences.

3.2.1 Commonalities

All the improvement management methods dealt with in the book are based on a holistic view of the entire process flow. They look beyond departmental boundaries and partly even beyond company boundaries and thus fully uncover the existing optimisation potential. This allows the various interdependent work processes to be ideally aligned with each other. This leads to an overarching optimised process system that contributes to the more efficient management of the entire company.

With the exception of business reengineering, all the methods described are based on the same basic attitude. This includes, in particular, a cooperative corporate culture, a focus on customers, continuous development of work processes and the strong involvement of the employees concerned in the improvement process. In addition, the anchoring of process thinking and the corresponding improvement culture in the entire organisation as well as a strong commitment of the management is a prerequisite.

The use of a visual component is another common feature of the various methods (except business reengineering). Whether it be in the visualisation of irregularities in the work processes by means of the corresponding charts or in the joint processing of the improvement projects with the help of various tools for visual representation. These include, for example, Process Mapping or the Ishikawa Diagram. These two tools are described in more detail in Sects. 4.1.6 and 4.1.7.

3.2.2 Differences

Although the various improvement methods are based on comparable principles and the same historical basis, they still differ greatly from each other in some cases. For example, while Kaizen focuses on continuous improvement in small steps, business reengineering relies on a radical redesign of essential work processes. This inevitably leads to completely different approaches in the processing and implementation of the individual optimisations.

There are major differences between the methods, especially in terms of processing time and effort. For example, optimisations according to the team-oriented CIP method are realised in short team workshops of half a day to a maximum of 1 day, while in the Six Sigma method, the improvements are tackled in a project organisation over several weeks.

Likewise, the various methods differ greatly in the way they deal with daily challenges. Agile methods such as Scrum rely on independent and self-organising teams of experts with a high degree of creative freedom, while, for example, Six Sigma places great importance on clear processes with the corresponding guidelines, checklists and regular measurements of predefined key figures.

Figure 3.18 shows an overview of the methods dealt with and a comparison of the main characteristics.

Criteria	Improvement method				
	Team-oriented CIP	Kaizen	Six Sigma	Business Reengineering	Agile methods
Origin / Founder	Analogue Kaizen with a focus on the team	After World War 2 at Toyota by Taiichi Ohno	Around 1990 at Motorola by Bill Smith	Around 1990 by Michael Hammer and James Champy	Around 1990 based on the Agile Manifesto
Use	To optimise the processes in your own team	To optimise overarching workflows	To optimise overarching workflows	For the redesign of workflows	For the management of innovation projects and projects
Impact	Optimisation of cooperation in the team	More efficient customer-focused workflows	More efficient and measurable customer-focused operations	Processes redefined from scratch	Efficient and timely control of projects
Implementation effort	small	medium	high	high	medium
Achievable benefit	small	medium	high	high	medium
Solution finding	In own team	In workshops with the employees concerned	In projects with the employees concerned	In a project with specialists and external support	In specialised teams
Tools	Simple tools (example brainstorming)	Process mapping to record the process and other tools	Various tools with a strong focus on numbers and measurement	Tools for the structured handling of the project	Various tools for visualisation (e.g., burndown chart)
Involvement of employees	Yes - own team	Yes - employees involved in the workflow	Yes - employees involved in the workflow	No	Yes - Teams involved in implementation
Disadvantages	Only internal team issues are optimised. External interfaces are not considered.	Optimisation is based on existing processes. Radical adjustments are thus hardly possible.	Optimisation is based on existing processes. Radical adjustments are thus hardly possible.	The existing is "thrown overboard". This also means that a lot of know-how is lost.	Primarily suitable for new product developments and the implementation of projects.

Fig. 3.18 Comparison of the different improvement methods

3.2.3 Other Methods

In addition to the improvement methods described before, there are many other approaches to improving work processes. These have become more or less established under different names and designations. Often these approaches are strongly based on the methods described in the book and hence differ only slightly from them. The most pervasive are briefly described here:

Lean Management

The notion of lean management pertains to the corporate management and pursues the goal of minimising waste and optimally coordinating the various work processes. This is to be achieved through process-oriented corporate management with clearly defined processes and procedures. The focus is on production. Lean management is heavily based on the Kaizen method.

Lean Administration

Lean administration focuses primarily on the work processes in administration. It originates from lean management, which is, however, more strongly oriented towards industrial production. The focus is on eliminating waste in work processes with the aim of making them more effective and efficient. Like lean management, lean administration is heavily based on the Kaizen method.

Total Quality Management

Total quality management aims at a permanent optimisation of processes, whereby quality is of central importance. Quality is not only the quality of the products and services produced but also the quality of the processes and the working conditions.

Total quality management also pursues a continuous improvement of existing work processes with the involvement of the employees concerned. The method, which originates from quality management, is based on the findings of William E. Deming and his Deming Circle.

EFQM Model

Thanks to a standardised assessment of the individual influencing factors, the EFQM model allows for a meaningful comparison of the quality of different companies. This independent assessment serves as the basis for the European Quality Award (EFQM Excellence Award) and other quality awards.

The EFQM model was developed in Europe in 1988 and has its roots in quality management. With the model, which focuses strongly on continuous improvement, a holistic optimisation of the organisation is pursued. The focus is on the three pillars: enablers, processes and results.

ISO Certificates

ISO represents a quality management standard which is used to certify companies or parts of companies. ISO certifications are performed by independent certification bodies. The certified companies are attested as complying with the required standards. In certain industries, ISO certification is an essential prerequisite for the successful distribution of the products and services produced.

The ISO quality management standards focus on a process-based organisation in which the continuous improvement of work processes with the involvement of the employees concerned plays an important role.

3.3 Selection of the Most Suitable Method

It is not absolutely necessary to strictly follow the same improvement method for all optimisations in the company. Instead, it is essential that the basic attitude of continuous improvement is anchored and lived. The different characteristics of the various improvement methods offer the possibility in everyday life to choose the appropriate method depending on the complexity of the problem and to place it in the overall context of internal improvement management.

When choosing an improvement method for dealing with an improvement topic, it is crucial to compare the costs and benefits beforehand. Workshops according to the Kaizen method, for example, require the commitment of several working days of each employee involved. In order to justify this effort, the result of the workshop must be a correspondingly large improvement. As a general rule, only complex cross-team and cross-departmental issues with a correspondingly large benefit justify more costly Kaizen workshops or Six Sigma projects.

3.3.1 Benefit Versus Costs

It is important that not only the reduction of costs is regarded as an improvement. Other aspects such as customer satisfaction, employee satisfaction, better product quality, etc. must also be taken into account in the evaluation of benefits. Figure 3.19 shows the comparison of benefits versus costs of improvement projects.

The decisive factor is that the expected benefit from the optimisation of the workflow exceeds the processing and implementation costs. Otherwise, it makes no sense, at least from a business point of view, to tackle and implement the improvement project in the planned form.

Since the benefit cannot always be measured in monetary units, the cost-benefit analysis is a suitable tool for an objective assessment of the benefit and the cost of an improvement project. The cost-benefit analysis is described in detail in Sect. 4.1.10.

> **Recommended Reading** Toyota's rise to a global corporation began after World War II. The Kaizen method, which was developed by Taiichi Ohno, Toyota's production manager, played a significant role in this. In the book *The Toyota Production System*, Taiichi Ohno (2019) impressively describes his experiences with the introduction of the method at Toyota.

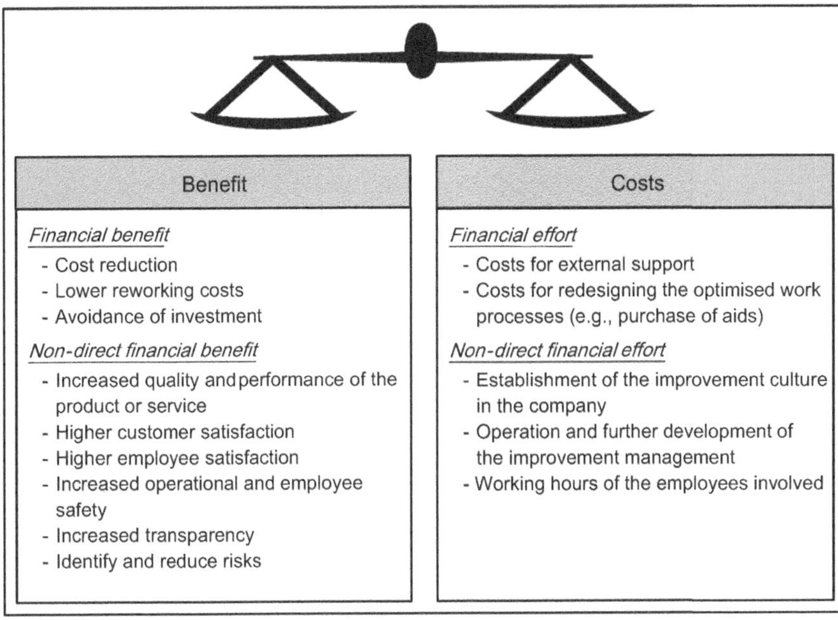

Fig. 3.19 Benefits versus costs of improvement projects

References

Agilemanifeste.org. (2001). *The 12 principles of the Agile Manifesto*. Retrieved 17 of December 2020 from http://agilemanifeste.org/iso/de/principles.html

Deming, W. (2018). *Out of the crisis*. Cambridge, MA: Massachusetts Institute of Technology.

Hammer, M., & Champy, J. (1993). *Reengineering the corporation: A manifesto for business revolution*. New York: Harper Business.

Knecht, A., & Bertschi, M. (2013). *Six sigma tools – beispiele – praxistipps*. Zürich: Versus.

Lunau St. (Hrsg.) (2014). *Six Sigma + Lean Toolset: Mindset zur erfolgreichen Umsetzung von Verbesserungsprojekten*. Berlin: Springer.

Ohno, T. (2019). *The Toyota production system*. Productivity Press.

Roock, St., & Wolf, H. (2016). *Scrum verstehen und erfolgreich einsetzen*. Heidelberg: dpunkt. verlag.

Töpfer, A. (2009). *Lean six sigma: Erfolgreiche Kombination von Lean management, six sigma und design for six sigma*. Berlin: Springer.

Tools for the Optimisation of Workflows

4

Tools to Optimise Workflows

When working on improvement projects, the use of different tools has a positive effect on the achievement of goals. All of these tools rely on a strong visual component, which is ideal for use in workshops with groups. This chapter provides an overview of the most important tools and shows where and how they are used.

The Maturity Model

The Maturity Model provides a structured procedure for assessing the quality of existing work processes as well as for tracking the progress made in continuous development. The Maturity Model is presented, and its application demonstrated.

Practical Experience of an Expert on the Maturity Model

Kateryna Brönnimann has introduced the Maturity Model in a company. She reports on her experiences during the development and introduction in the company.

M. Hofmann, *A Holistic Approach to Process Optimisation*, Management for Professionals, https://doi.org/10.1007/978-3-658-34097-1_4

4.1 Tools for the Optimisation of Workflows

After the most important improvement methods, their characteristics and different areas of application were presented in Chaps. 3 and 4 focuses on the most important tools that are used in the context of processing and implementing improvement projects. Here, it is interesting to note that most of these tools were not developed specifically for the improvement of work processes. Some of them have been around for much longer and were developed to solve a wide variety of problems in different fields. With the increasing prevalence of the various improvement methods in the last century, these tools found a new use. In the context of developing and implementing an increase in efficiency, they are used to process the tasks that arise.

These tools serve as important aids and support a targeted and structured process when working on improvement projects. Thus, they contribute significantly to the successful development of optimisations. The most important advantages of using these tools are, among other things, the simple handling, the structured procedure and the clear visual presentation. This makes it easier for all participants to keep the overview in comprehensive workshops and promotes cooperation. As Fig. 4.1 shows, only a few simple aids are needed to work with these tools.

In order to use the documents jointly developed in the workshop for further processing later on, and to be able to transport them easily, rolls of brown paper or detachable sheets of a flipchart, for example, serve as an ideal work surface. This also simplifies the later documentation of the results, although I recommend the use of photographic records for reasons of efficiency. Here, it is important to ensure that the content of the photos remains legible. Differently coloured self-adhesive notes (post-its) as well as pens in different colours and with different thicknesses are sufficient to visualise the contents. In my experience, this work method has various advantages compared to recording everything directly in computer programmes. Documenting it electronically may be quicker and more efficient, but it leads to a poorer group dynamic. Creativity suffers and it is more difficult to involve all participants equally.

The development and implementation of improvement projects is one thing, the measurement of benefit and effect is another. For this purpose, the Maturity Model is presented at the end of the chapter. This tool is used to assess the quality of work

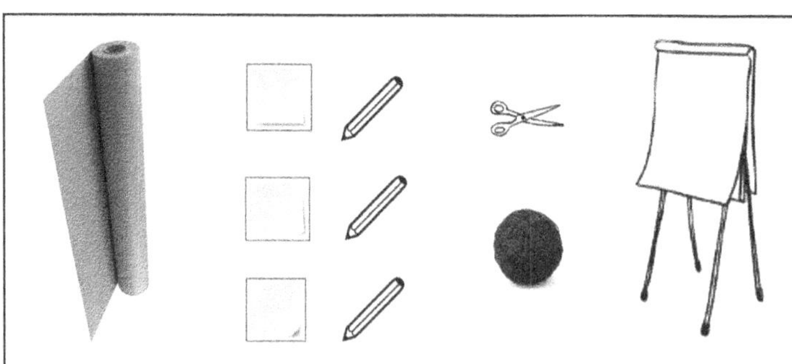

Fig. 4.1 Aids for the application of the tools

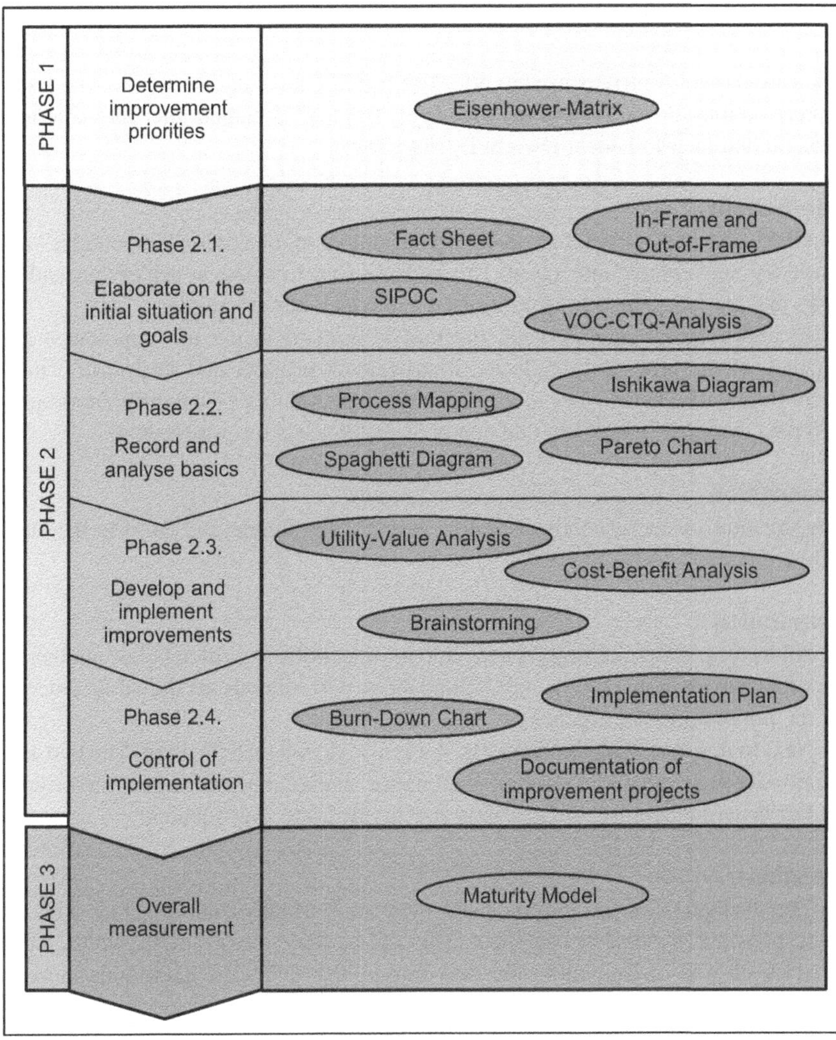

Fig. 4.2 Tools by phase of improvement

processes in the company. It enables an overall comparison between organisational units and their work processes and provides new inputs for future improvement projects at the same time.

Overview of the Most Important Tools

There is a wide range of tools that can be used to tackle improvement projects. Figure 4.2 gives an overview of the most common tools that are used in the individual phases of improvement.

All the tools listed in the overview are briefly described on the following pages. In addition, the practical application is shown by means of examples.

4.1.1 Eisenhower-Matrix

The Eisenhower-Matrix is used to prioritise pending tasks and activities. The visual representation allows for a quick overview. The tool is named after the American General and later President Dwight D. Eisenhower.

Use/Benefit

Pending tasks and activities are evaluated according to the criteria "importance" and "urgency" and entered into a grid. This makes it easy to assess which of the pending tasks and activities need to be prioritised and which are less urgent.

In improvement management, the tool is used to gauge the importance and urgency of the previously collected improvement projects and to prioritise them accordingly. The benefit lies in the resulting comparability of the different projects and the creation of a uniform and comprehensible basis for prioritisation.

Description

The creation of an Eisenhower-Matrix is relatively simple and follows the steps below:

Preparation

1. All the improvement projects available for selection are written below another on a flipchart as shown in Fig. 4.3. Behind them, two columns are drawn for entering the importance and urgency.
2. Next to it, a matrix as shown in Fig. 4.4 is also drawn on a flipchart. The two axes are labelled with the criteria of importance (horizontal) and urgency (vertical). For better readability, the matrix is also divided into four squares.

Creation

3. The evaluation of the improvement projects is usually done together with the responsible division management. This can be done, for example, with a rating scale of 1 to 6. Regarding the two criteria, the following definitions must be observed:
   - Importance: Importance is to be understood in the context of benefits. Important projects improve the existing process. As soon as an improvement is implemented, lasting benefits are achieved, or disadvantages are eliminated.

Initiatives	Description	Importance	Urgency
1	Simplify and standardise planning tools	5	4
2	Standardisation of product descriptions for shipping	4	2
3	Simplify ordering of internal office supplies	2	2
4	Simplify the online customer ordering process	6	5

Fig. 4.3 Evaluation of improvement projects

Fig. 4.4 Eisenhower-Matrix

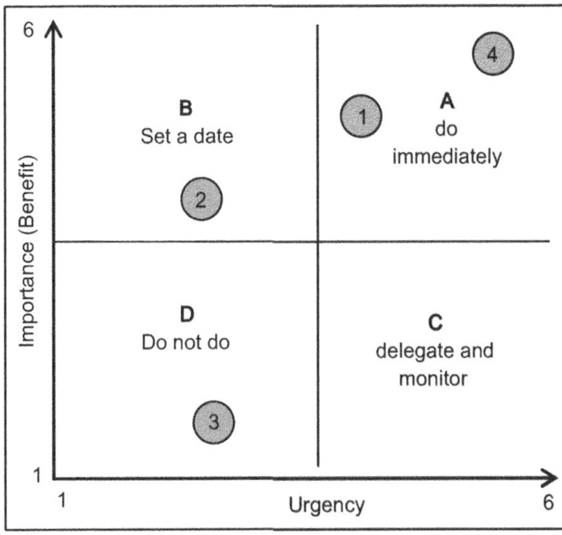

- Urgency: Urgency is to be understood in terms of time. A delay in urgent projects causes strong repercussions (for example: introduction of new products in two months or new contractual obligation regarding the error rate towards a customer). If the deadline is met, a benefit is gained, or damage is prevented.

4. After the assessment, each project is entered into the matrix. For this purpose, a dot is drawn at the point that represents the assessment of its 'importance' and 'urgency'. The finished Eisenhower-Matrix is to be interpreted as follows: The more important and urgent a project is, the faster it should be implemented. The division into four squares of equal size simplifies the placement on the matrix and further increases readability. These squares are to be interpreted as follows:

A. *Do immediately*: These are projects of great importance and urgency. Therefore, their processing should be given the highest priority.
B. *Set a date:* These projects also provide great benefits but are somewhat less time sensitive. It is important that these projects are scheduled, and the implementation is approached accordingly.
C. *Delegate and monitor:* The benefits of these projects are smaller and usually do not justify a large investment of resources. Therefore, these projects are directly assigned to an affected team. A simple team workshop, for example, is suitable for processing them.
D. *Do not do:* These projects have very low importance and no time urgency. Hence, these projects should not be pursued further.

Example

In the retail sector of a supplier for the hotel industry, four concrete improvement projects have been submitted by the employees. These are discussed and evaluated together with the sales management. Figure 4.3 shows the result of the discussion.

Next, these four projects are entered into the Eisenhower-Matrix. Here, the assessment of 'importance' and 'urgency' serves as the basis for determining the position in the matrix. Figure 4.4 shows the completed Eisenhower-Matrix.

The completed Eisenhower-Matrix shows that projects one and four are of great importance and have a high degree of urgency at the same time. Therefore, these two projects should be tackled quickly. Project 3, on the other hand, appears to be neither important nor urgent. Therefore, this project should not be realised.

Tips and Tricks

1. For the acceptance of the results, it is helpful to involve the responsible management at an early stage and to carry out the evaluation of the individual topics together in a meeting in advance.
2. As an expression of appreciation to the idea providers, it is important that all of them receive timely feedback. This also applies if the project is not pursued further. In this case, it is important that the reason is communicated.
3. When prioritising the projects and subsequently scheduling them, the availability of the employees involved in the improvement must also be considered.

4.1.2 Fact Sheet

The fact sheet is used to map the key parameters of an improvement project. Most improvement methods use this tool in one form or another. In practice, the fact sheet exists in many different forms. The essential aspect of it is that the most important key parameters of the improvement project are presented in a comprehensible way on one or two pages.

Use/Benefit

The fact sheet is used to prepare for workshops or improvement projects and helps to promote a common understanding of the starting position and objectives for all participants. The great benefit of a fact sheet is that the starting position and the expectations of the sponsor are clearly defined beforehand and a common understanding is created for all those involved. This allows for an efficient and targeted approach to the development of optimisations.

Description

The fact sheet is created jointly by the coach and the sponsor. The points to be described in the fact sheet are:

Initial Situation/Problem Description

This section contains a detailed description of the current situation and the existing difficulties in the process. This promotes a common understanding of the current situation and forms the common basis for the workshop or improvement project.

Delimitation

Here, the problem points that are to be optimised are clearly described. It is crucial that the problem areas that will not be addressed are also clearly defined. This is important in order to define the focus and to tackle the essential points.

Goal/Effect

Here, the aspired goals and the expected effect are to be specified. For traceability and for subsequent measurement of the achievement of objectives, it makes sense to formulate objectives according to the 'SMART method'. The letters stand for 'Specific', 'Measurable', 'Achievable', 'Reasonable' and 'Time-bound'.

Participants

The employees involved in the workshop or improvement project must be identified by name and their availability must be ensured before the release of the fact sheet. The employees involved can be divided into the following three groups:

- *The sponsor:* They are responsible for the implementation of the improvement topic. They support the team in case of difficulties such as resource bottlenecks or coordination with other areas or process owners. They define the fact sheet

together with the coach and are responsible for its acceptance. They are present at the kick-off and the presentation of the results.
- *The coach:* They lead the workshop or the improvement project. Together with the sponsor, they are responsible for the creation of the fact sheet and ensure that the results are implemented. In addition, they conduct a review with all the participants a few weeks after completion and prepare a final report.
- *The participants:* They consist of the employees involved in the workflow from the different areas of the company. The ideal number of participants depends on the method chosen and the number of people involved in the process. However, the group should not consist of more than eight participants. With a larger group, leadership becomes burdensome and the focus is often lost.

Implementation
This is where the organisational framework conditions are defined. It must be noted here that the implementation strongly depends on the chosen method. While with Kaizen the implementation takes place in a workshop lasting several days, Six Sigma relies on a project that can take several weeks. It is important that the processing of an improvement project does not drag on for too long and that the measures taken are implemented quickly. It is also advisable to present the results achieved to all interested parties at the end. This helps the team to reflect on the output again, and it provides a good platform to communicate the results.

Sponsor's Signature
The signature is seen as a symbol that the basis for the improvement measures has been approved and that the actual work in the team can begin. Before giving the signature, it is the sponsor's task to confer with all the stakeholders and to resolve conflicting goals.

Example

Figure 4.5 shows a possible layout of a fact sheet. This can be adapted to the needs of the company. It should present the essential points clearly on one A4 page.

Tips and Tricks

1. It is very important that the fact sheet is created together with the sponsor. In addition, it is crucial that the sponsor plays a significant role in the company and thus gives the project the necessary weight.
2. For larger and more complex issues with many stakeholders, it makes sense to divide the improvement topic into several smaller topic sections and create several sub-sheets accordingly.
3. In my experience, when creating a fact sheet, it makes sense to concentrate on the essential points and to present them clearly on one page. Fact sheets that are too extensive are time-consuming to prepare and often contain unnecessary details.

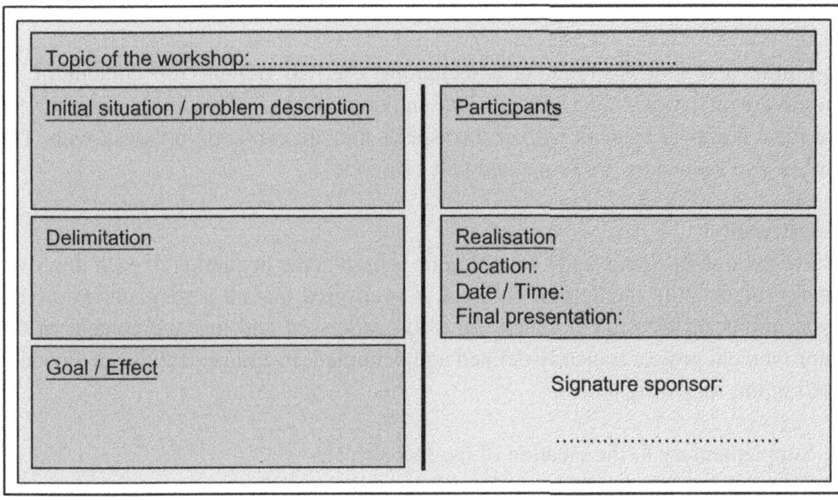

Fig. 4.5 Fact sheet

4.1.3 In-Frame and Out-of-Frame

In-Frame and Out-of-Frame is a technique used to delimit the content of an improvement project. The visual representation allows for a simple overview of the focal points to be dealt with or the aspects that are explicitly not dealt with. The tool is also known as 'In-Scope and Out-of-Scope'.

Use/Benefit

The technique In-Frame and Out-of-Frame is used at the beginning of each improvement project. With the help of this tool, it is ensured that all participants know the focal points of the project which are to be addressed and that the content of the improvement project is clearly defined and delimited. In-Frame and Out-of-Frame is used in the following cases:

1. Supplementary to the creation of the fact sheet
   The tool In-Frame and Out-of-Frame is applied together with the sponsor in the preparation phase as a supplement to the fact sheet. This supports the drafting of the fact sheet and enables a precise formulation of the item 'delimitation'. Thus, it allows for clear definition of the sub-aspects to be dealt with even before the start of the improvement project.
2. As an introduction at the start of the implementation together with the employees involved
   The tool can be created either before the workshop or at the beginning of the implementation together with the staff involved. The advantage of creating it together is that the common understanding of the problem is strengthened and a common basis for the following activities in the team is created. There is a risk that the delimitation defined in the team does not correspond to the sponsor's idea. For this reason, it is advisable to consult with the sponsor after the development of the tool In-Frame and Out-of-Frame.

   The creation of the tool is relatively simple. It is crucial that all essential sub-aspects are taken into account and that the result is supported by those involved (sponsor and employees). Otherwise, there is a risk that a wrong focus may be set.

Description

To create the tool In-Frame and Out-of-Frame, proceed as follows:

Preparation

1. Before the actual creation, a grid is drawn on a poster and hung on the wall. The grid is shown in Fig. 4.6.

Creation

2. Together with the employees involved, all possible partial aspects that are derived from the issue the improvement project is concerned with are collected and

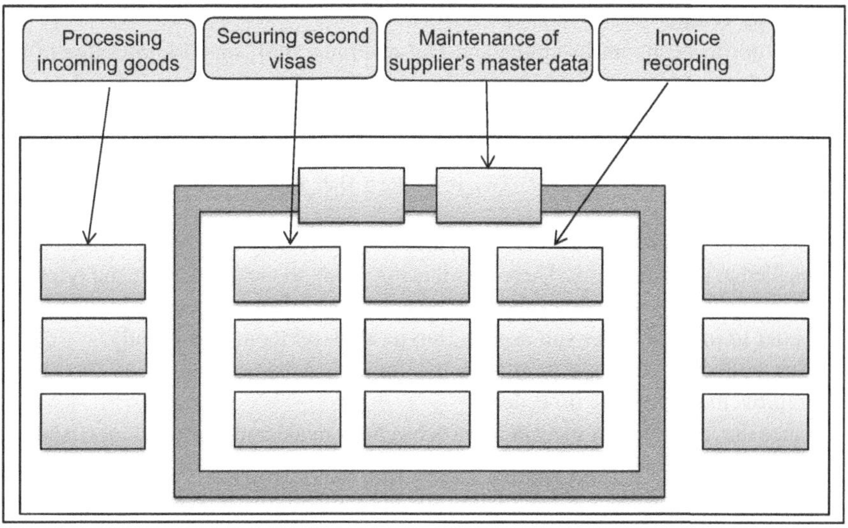

Fig. 4.6 In-Frame and Out-of-Frame

written individually on a card. This can be done in a brainstorming session, for instance. The cards are pinned onto a wall so that they are clearly visible.

3. To promote common understanding and to avoid misunderstandings, the collected entries are discussed. At the same time, the partial aspects entered are checked for duplicates.
4. Next, it is decided for each partial aspect whether it is part of the focus of the improvement project. Aspects that are to be dealt with within the project are stuck inside the frame of the tool. Aspects that are not to be dealt with are stuck outside the frame. If there is any uncertainty regarding the delimitation, the topic is stuck onto the frame. Afterwards, it is decided in consultation with the sponsor whether these points are part of the focus of the improvement project or not.

Example

In the accounting department of a trading company, an In-Frame and Out-of-Frame tool is created together with the sponsor of the improvement project on the topic of 'more efficient processing of incoming supplier invoices'. Figure 4.6 shows how the recorded sub-aspects are entered into the tool.

The structure of the In-Frame and Out-of-Frame tool can be easily demonstrated using this example. The sub-aspect 'Securing second visas' is within the focus of the improvement project and is to be worked on accordingly. In contrast, the sub-aspect 'Processing incoming goods' is not within the focus and therefore does not need to be worked on. In the case of the sub-aspect 'Maintenance of supplier's master data', the allocation cannot yet be finalised. This sub-aspect will be assessed again together with the sponsor in a later phase after the first in-depth findings are available.

Tips and Tricks

1. In order to create an In-Frame and Out-of-Frame tool, sound knowledge of the workflow under consideration is necessary. Therefore, the creation is often only possible together with the staff involved. In my experience, it is very important in this case to agree on the delimitations made with the sponsor before continuing to work on the project. Otherwise, there is a risk that the wrong topics will be dealt with.
2. Improvement projects are often extensive and too many different sub-aspects are tackled at the same time. Therefore, it is important to clearly delimit and prioritise the project with the help of the In-Frame and Out-of-Frame tool. If in doubt, it is better to include fewer sub-aspects, but to work on them consistently.
3. The collected sub-aspects outside the frame can be used as ideas for further improvement projects if needed.
4. Once the allocation of the sub-aspects has been made and approved together with the sponsor, it should not be changed during the handling of the improvement project. A subsequent adjustment of the delimitation often leads to uncertainties, duplications and extra work.

4.1.4 SIPOC

The SIPOC diagram is used to clearly depict the most important interrelationships of an overall process. This tool supports the definition and delimitation of a planned improvement project by clearly displaying the most important components of the workflow under consideration, including the required inputs and the created outputs. The input providers (suppliers) and output recipients (customers) involved in the process are also identified and mapped.

This tool originally stems from the Six Sigma method. However, it is now widely used in various other improvement methods as well.

Use/Benefit

The SIPOC diagram is used as a starting point for working on an improvement project and is intended to provide an initial overview of the workflow to be improved. With the help of the SIPOC diagram, the overarching dependencies of the process are revealed and the common understanding of the process to be worked on is promoted. The graphical representation of the workflow creates transparency in terms of process composition and identifies the suppliers and the customers. The abbreviation SIPOC stands for the following terms:

- *S—Supplier:* Stands for the supplier who provides the required input for the corresponding process step. Both external and internal suppliers are considered and included.
- *I—Input:* Stands for the necessary input information. This can comprise materials, resources, information or documents that are needed in the corresponding process step.
- *P—Process:* This item represents the actual processing operation within the workflow and involves the transformation of the input to the output. These are the actual activities within the workflow.
- *O—Output:* Stands for the product or service that is provided to the internal or external customer. This is often a partial product or information that is needed in a subsequent work step.
- *C—Customer:* Stands for the purchaser of the output generated in the corresponding process step. Both internal and external recipients of services are considered customers.

Description

The SIPOC diagram is preferably drawn up on a large sheet of paper attached to the wall and is presented in the form of a table. The table is filled in together with the staff involved. The following steps are taken:

1. First, the headings (Supplier, Input, Process, Output and Customer) are written on five cards and pinned side by side onto the brown paper.

2. Then, together with the employees involved, the start and end points of the workflow under consideration are determined. These are written on cards and pasted in the column 'Process'.
3. The next step is to record the individual process steps that take place between the start and end points. If there is no current process documentation, the easiest way to identify them is by brainstorming. They are listed under the heading 'Process' in the order in which they are executed. To maintain clarity, only the five to eight most important process steps are shown.
4. After the process steps have been defined, the following are determined for the individual process steps in this specific order: Output, Customer, Input and Supplier.

Example

As an example of the creation of a SIPOC diagram, let's look at the offer creation by a craft business which, among other things, carries out painting work for private customers. The starting point of the process is the receipt of the customer's request by the customer service. The end point is the transmission of the offer to the customer. The other process steps required for the offer creation are 'check availability' and 'finalise offer'.

After the essential process steps have been determined and listed in the SIPOC diagram, the missing information for each individual step is entered into the table. For the process step '*check availability*', for example, this is the following information:

- *Shop Manager under Supplier:* This is the person responsible for planning the employees' assignments.
- *Possible dates under Input:* All dates of the employees still available for the execution of the desired task.
- *Date suggestion under Output:* This is the specific time for carrying out the painting work after checking the availability of the employees and in coordination with the customer's request.
- *Customer Service under Customer:* The date suggestion under output is transferred to customer service for further processing.

The fully completed SIPOC diagram with the individual process steps and the corresponding information is shown in Fig. 4.7.

Tips and Tricks

1. When creating the SIPOC diagram, it is crucial to keep the right level of detail. It does not make sense to elaborate too much.
2. When recording the individual sub-processes, it makes sense to always start with the customer and the output, and only then fill in the remaining boxes. This way, the procedure focuses on the customer and their needs.
3. After the completion of the SIPOC diagram, it is important that the lessons learned are aligned with the framework and objectives of the improvement

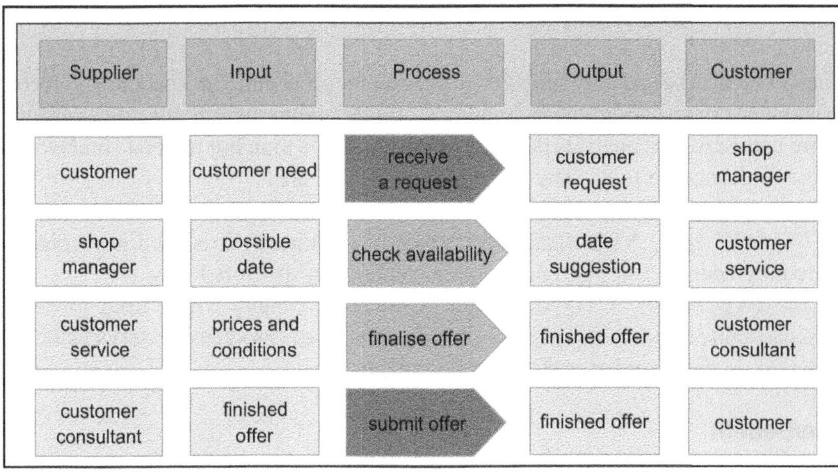

Fig. 4.7 SIPOC diagram

project. If these differ, it must be examined whether the framework of the project was set correctly. If necessary, the process delimitation in the SIPOC diagram should be checked again and adjusted if necessary.

4.1.5 VOC-CTQ-Analysis

The VOC-CTQ-Analysis supports a structured procedure to specifically record existing customer requirements and transform them into measurable core concerns. More precisely, this analysis does not involve a single tool, but rather a combination of two independent tools. The two tools in question are:

- *The VOC table:* VOC stands for 'Voice of Customer'. It is used to record the requirements, wishes and needs of customers in a structured way.
- *The CTQ matrix:* CTQ stands for 'Critical to Quality'. It is used to define measurable quality requirements for the processes, products or services and is based on the recorded customer requirements.

Use/Benefit

These two tools, which are actually independent, can be excellently combined to allow customer requirements to be directly incorporated in the creation process. Both internal and external customer requirements are included. This is done by recording the requirements, wishes and needs of the customers and anchoring them as measurable criteria in the corresponding workflow.

Figure 4.8 shows how the key topics obtained from the VOC table are transferred to the CTQ matrix, where they are condensed into the essential requirements.

The result of the VOC-CTQ-Analysis is the core concerns of internal and external customers derived from the customer requirements. In addition, corresponding measurement criteria and their target values are defined for all core concerns.

Description

A VOC-CTQ-Analysis is conducted in two independent steps together with the employees involved in the process. The procedure is as follows:

Part 1: Creating the VOC Table

In the first part, the VOC table is created:

1. The first step is to determine the most important internal and external customers. These can be derived from the SIPOC diagram, for example.
2. Subsequently, the identified customers are asked about their requirements, wishes and needs. This can be done by means of interviews or written surveys. In

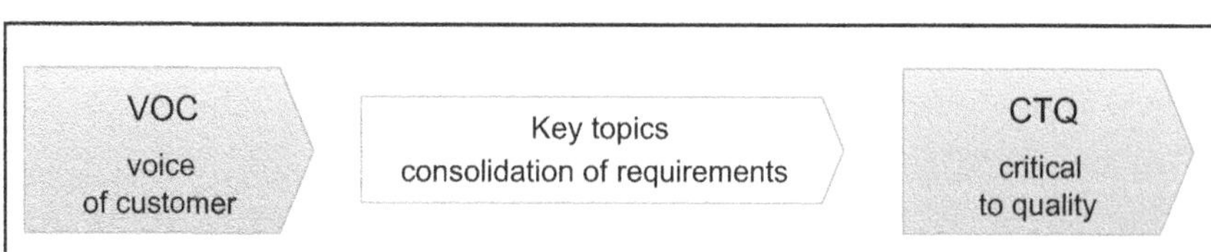

Fig. 4.8 Overview Structure VOC-CTQ-Analysis

addition, nowadays new possibilities for identifying customer requirements arise in connection with data acquisition from digitalisation.
3. The central customer needs are derived from the collected feedback from the customers and entered into the VOC table.
4. Finally, the recorded customer needs are prioritised according to their importance.

Part 2: Deriving the CTQ Matrix
In the second part, the CTQ matrix is created. This is also done together with the staff involved and according to the following steps:

1. The relevant key topics are filtered out of the finished VOC table and transferred to the CTQ matrix as essential requirements.
2. The core concerns are derived from the essential requirements and also entered into the CTQ matrix.
3. Finally, measurable quality requirements are defined for the core concerns. These are used to monitor the corresponding processes or the products produced.

Example

The following example of an insurance company handling claims illustrates the procedure for preparing a VOC-CTQ-Analysis.

In the customer survey conducted, the long time it takes to settle claims and the constantly changing contact persons are among the negative aspects mentioned. Derived from this are the central starting points for optimising the process, including the key measurement points. The complete VOC-CTQ-Analysis is shown in Fig. 4.9.

VOC - recording			
customer	existing challenge	customer wishes and needs	priority
A	Preparation of the statement takes a very long time	The customer wants a quick settlement of his claim	1
B	Was contacted by various employees	The customer wants acompetent contact person	2

Condensing the statements into essential requirements

CTQ- analysis			
essential requirements	core concerns	CTQ	priority
Rapid claims settlement	Efficient settlement process	Number of days for claims settlement	1
A competent contact person	One contact person per customer	Number of customer contacts per claim	2

Fig. 4.9 VOC-CTQ-Analysis

Tips and Tricks

1. To prevent the distortion of customer statements during interviews, it is important that the statements are recorded verbatim.
2. Customer statements alone do not provide added value. It is crucial that these are bundled into meaningful customer requirements and that corresponding quality criteria are defined. It is particularly important that these are tangible and measurable.
3. Before further processing, it is helpful to discuss the findings from the VOC-CTQ-Analysis with the sponsor of the improvement project. Possible ambiguities can thus be identified and eliminated at an early stage.

4.1.6 Process Mapping

Process Mapping is a tool for visually representing an existing workflow and determining existing fields of action. The individual work steps are assigned to the roles involved (persons or departments). Process Mapping is also known by other names in slightly different forms. The most common ones are: Process Flow Diagram, Value-Stream Mapping or Swimlane Diagram.

Use/Benefit

Process Mapping is used for the precise representation of existing work processes. It is also suitable for determining concrete fields of action to increase efficiency and quality. The actual benefit of this tool lies in the visual representation of the interrelationships within the process. It illustrates the interaction of all those involved, including the existing interfaces within and outside the workflow. In addition, it becomes clear which work steps add value and which work steps contain waste. By measuring the time spent on the individual activities, further insights into the efficiency of the process can be gained. A distinction is made between lead time and processing time.

▶ **Lead Time** Is the total time measured from the receipt of an input to an outgoing output for an activity. Accordingly, the lead time also includes waiting and idle times.

▶ **Processing Time** Is the pure working time that is used for the performance of the actual activity.

Based on the recorded actual-condition-analyses, the Process Mapping can also be used to define the target processes. For this purpose, the adjustments decided on in the improvement project are incorporated into the process accordingly.

Description

Process Mapping is time-consuming depending on the complexity of the workflow under consideration and can take up to one day. The employees concerned should be involved in the creation of the map, as they know the processes best. The following procedure is used for the creation:

Preparation

1. A brown paper is hung on the wall as a work surface. On it, the basic lines of the grid are drawn according to Fig. 4.10.
2. Cards, pens and tape are prepared. Ideally, differently coloured cards are used for the different categories.

Creation

3. First, the boundaries of the workflow to be documented must be defined. This means determining where and with what input the process begins and where and

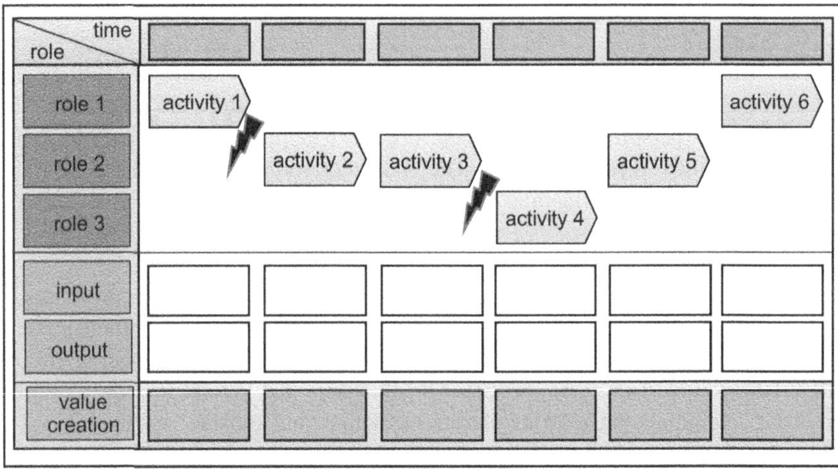

Fig. 4.10 Process Mapping

with what output it ends. This information can be derived from a SIPOC diagram, for instance.

4. Next, the roles involved in the process are named. These are each written on a card and pasted below another in the first column of the Process Mapping.
5. Then, the individual work steps within the process are recorded. These are also written on cards and attributed to the executing role in the order in which they are carried out. At the same time, the inputs and outputs of the respective work step are recorded and also pasted onto the brown paper.
6. Next, it is determined for each activity whether it is value adding or wasteful. Value creation and waste in work processes are described in detail in Sect. 1.3.
7. In the next step, the processing and lead time per activity is recorded and noted above the corresponding work steps. These times add up to the total processing or lead time of the workflow.
8. Finally, all existing fields of action of the workflow under consideration are recorded on the brown paper with a red lightning bolt. These can be, for example, unclear interfaces, missing work instructions, time overlaps, missing inputs or unclear outputs.

Example

The structure of the Process Mapping is shown in Fig. 4.10.

Tips and Tricks

1. When creating the Process Mapping, there is a danger of slipping into a wishful image instead of depicting the current situation. To prevent this, it is important to observe the workflow on site and to only document it afterwards.
2. From my own experience I can say that it is dangerous to estimate the lead and processing time. In order to avoid false results, it is important to measure the real

times on the spot. Attention: Special care should be taken not to forget small time wasters which occur irregularly (for example: revision of meeting documents because of subsequent inputs from the project leader).

3. It is particularly helpful to print out the documents used in each case (such as tables, templates, instructions or lists) for each work step and to hang them below the corresponding step. This makes inconsistencies and duplications in the workflow particularly visible.
4. Instead of the employees' names and specific departments, roles should always be used to designate the implementing agency. They are independent of the current organisation and the persons involved.
5. Let the participants write their own contributions and post them on the board: This encourages participation and reduces the burden on the coach.

4.1.7 Ishikawa Diagram (Fishbone Diagram)

The Ishikawa Diagram is used to identify the main causes of an existing problem. The graphical representation provides a simple overview and helps to classify the causes. The diagram was developed in the early 1950s by the Japanese scientist Kaoru Ishikawa as a method for analysing quality issues. Originally hailing from quality management, the Ishikawa Diagram is now frequently used in improvement management for the targeted analysis of the causes of errors.

The Ishikawa Diagram resembles a fishbone in its depiction, which is why it is often called a 'Fishbone Diagram'. It is also known as a 'Cause and Effect Diagram'.

Use/Benefit

This tool enables an in-depth analysis of a concrete problem or error. For this purpose, the underlying causes are determined and written on the respective main branch of the diagram. Each main branch embodies a cause category and serves to group the individual causes. In the standard diagram, the six main branches correspond to the following 6Ms (Men, Machine, Method, Material, Mother Nature (Environment) and Measurement). However, these do not necessarily have to be used. Depending on the problem, it may be useful to determine the cause categories yourself.

The Ishikawa Diagram is very suitable for use in a team CIP or an improvement workshop. It not only helps to find the causes of a problem, but also promotes a common understanding of the issue. Derived from the name 'Fishbone Diagram', the main branches of the cause categories are often called 'fishbones'. In addition, the box for stating the issue is also known as 'fish head'.

Description

The creation of the Ishikawa Diagram is ideally done in collaboration with the staff involved, as they know the current situation best. The creation takes place in the following steps:

Preparation

1. First, the template of the Ishikawa Diagram is drawn on a brown paper and pinned to the wall (see Fig. 4.11). The boxes for the issue and the individual cause categories remain empty for the time being.

Creation

2. The starting point for the joint meeting is the formulation of the main problem. It is important that all participants have a common understanding of the issue. This is written on a small card and placed in the "fish head" of the diagram.
3. Subsequently, the superordinate cause categories are determined and entered. If possible, the established 6Ms are to be used. This enables a uniform grouping of the cause categories in case of recurring usage.
4. The causes of the problem are worked out together in the team. Here, it is important to note that all possible causes must be assessed in terms of their effect

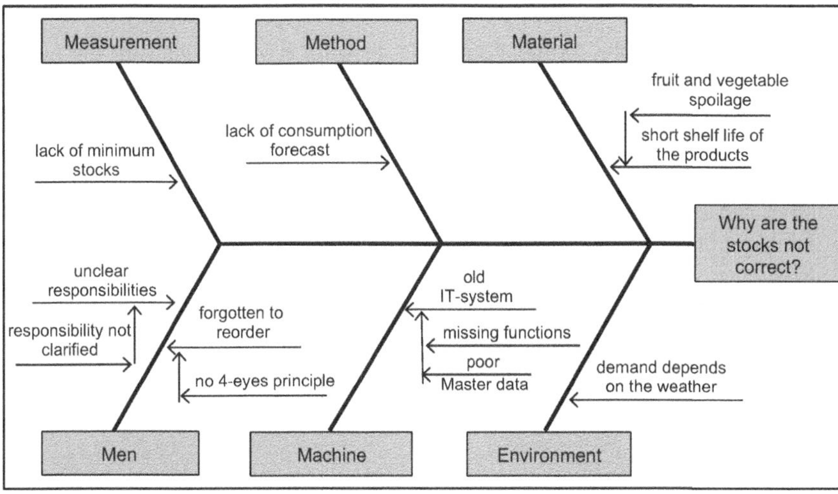

Fig. 4.11 Ishikawa Diagram

on the problem. A brainstorming session would be very suitable for recording the causes. This way it could be ensured that all those involved get a chance to speak and that the possible causes are recorded as comprehensively as possible.

5. Then the collected causes are examined again and formulated in detail. The 5 Whys technique is particularly suitable for this. According to this root cause analysis tool, all the causes recorded are further expanded on five times with the question 'why'. This allows the causes to be further specified and possibly divided into several sub-items. These sub-items are recorded as side branches in the diagram.
6. After the recording is completed, the causes are classified in terms of their capacity to influence and their influenceability. This classification shows which causes have the greatest influence on the problem and whether they can be influenced or not.
7. The recorded causes for the defined problem are then worked through together in the team in the order of their influence. In the process, ideas for solutions and measures to remedy the problem are determined.

Example

The customers of a grocery shop regularly complain about missing goods on the shelves. At the same time, goods regularly have to be destroyed because stocks are too high and the products spoil. For these reasons, the store manager conducts a workshop with the staff to identify the causes of the problem.

First, they jointly define the question: *Why are the stocks of goods on the shelf not correct?* Then they draw up an Ishikawa Diagram, which should provide the main causes for the defined issue. These causes can now be addressed and remedied with targeted measures. Figure 4.11 shows the finished Ishikawa Diagram.

Tips and Tricks

1. In my experience the formulation of the question is very crucial for the further processing of the problem. Therefore, it is important that all participants have understood what the existing problem is and that they agree with the formulation of the question.
2. The question should not be too multi-layered and complex. If necessary, it is advisable to divide the question into several sub-questions and to create a separate Ishikawa Diagram for each question.
3. When creating the Ishikawa Diagram, it is important that all relevant causes are recorded. Whether these are assigned to the correct cause criteria is not as crucial. Therefore, there should not be spent too much time on the exact allocation to the cause criteria.

4.1.8 Spaghetti Diagram

The Spaghetti Diagram is used to record and visually depict the distances travelled and the transports carried out in a very simple way. The finished depiction shows how often the employees observed go to a certain place and which walking distances they cover within the observation period.

The name Spaghetti Diagram is derived from the fact that the depiction often resembles a plate of spaghetti in its appearance.

Use/Benefit

The Spaghetti Diagram is used with the aim of revealing waste in existing work processes. For example, the two types of waste 'transport' and 'movement' can be easily recorded and visualised this way. On a sketch, which corresponds to the floor plan of the work area, the distances covered are drawn in the form of lines during a defined observation period. The paths of employees as well as the paths of materials and documents can be mapped.

The benefit of the Spaghetti Diagram lies both in revealing efficiency losses in existing work processes and in gaining interesting conclusions about a sensible layout of existing workplaces. Overall, the Spaghetti Diagram provides important starting points for reducing existing waste.

In principle, the more convoluted the lines are arranged on the Spaghetti Diagram created, the less productive the observed workflow is.

Description

To create a Spaghetti Diagram, proceed as follows:

Preparation

1. The first thing to do is to sketch the layout of the workplace. Here, it is important to make sure that this is drawn to scale. This enables a quantitative evaluation of the distances covered.
2. Next, the observation period for recording the diagram is determined. This period must be long enough to be able to make a reliable statement about the waste in the workflow.

Creation

3. During the observation period, a corresponding line for each path travelled is drawn in the prefabricated layout. Already during the observation, the first superfluous paths and optimisations can be recognised. Even if it becomes confusing, it is important for the later analysis that all paths are entered individually.
4. After recording the paths, the sketch created is analysed. Here, a distinction is to be made between a qualitative and a quantitative evaluation:
   - Qualitative evaluation: A single glance is sufficient for a qualitative evaluation of the diagram produced. If the diagram is extremely convoluted, a high

potential for improvement can be assumed. Long lines and especially thick clusters of lines in particular are signs of waste and potential for optimisation.
 - Quantitative evaluation: For a quantitative evaluation, the length of the individual lines is measured in order to calculate a total distance. For this, a simple table is helpful (see the example in Fig. 4.13).
5. Based on the insights gathered with the Spaghetti Diagram, the waste that has been uncovered can now be addressed and the existing efficiency losses can be eliminated in a targeted manner.

Example

The following example shows how a Spaghetti Diagram can be used to check the distances travelled by a management assistant for waste. To record the distances travelled, the assistant is observed for one hour. These distances travelled are transferred to the prepared layout shown in Fig. 4.12.

Already during the recording, it is noticeable that they are 'on the move' a lot and thus have to interrupt their work quite often. The subsequent transfer of the visual image into the evaluation table shows that the assistant was on the move a total of 18 times within one hour and covered 196 metres in the process. The complete evaluation table is shown in Fig. 4.13. It also becomes apparent that the workplace layout is not optimal as with a better layout, the distances could be shortened. Swapping the printer with the filing cabinet alone would save about a third of the distance.

Tips and Tricks

1. For better readability, it makes sense to either use individual Spaghetti Diagrams for different employees or to enter the paths with different colours.
2. For long workflows with many variables, the Spaghetti Diagram can become confusing very quickly. Therefore, it makes sense to limit oneself to the actual core question or to divide the question into different sub-questions and record them separately.

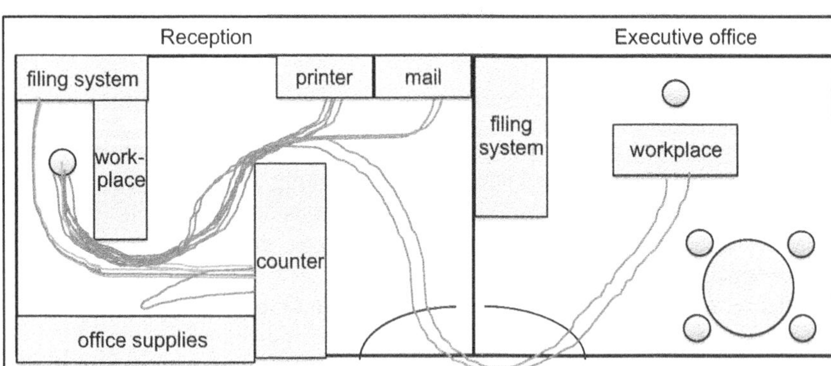

Fig. 4.12 Spaghetti Diagram

Spaghetti Diagram for assistance job Observation period: 1 hour				date: 20 march	
from place 1	to place 2	comment	distance	number of paths	total distance
workplace	counter		7 metres	4	28 metres
counter	office supplies		4 metres	2	8 metres
workplace	printer		10 metres	6	60 metres
workplace	mail		12 metres	2	24 metres
workplace	workplace boss		30 metres	2	60 metres
counter	filing system		8 metres	2	16 metres
				total distance	196 metres

Fig. 4.13 Spaghetti Diagram—evaluation table

3. The Spaghetti Diagram is also suitable for tracking goods, documents or working papers. This can provide interesting insights, especially in administration.

4.1.9 Pareto Chart

The Pareto Chart is used to visually represent the proportions of different groups of data. The representation is based on the Pareto principle with the 80/20 rule. This principle states that approximately 80% of the problems that occur are due to 20% of causes. The Pareto Chart is named after the Italian economist Vilfredo Pareto and is used in statistics, among other fields.

The chart shows the distribution of the different data groups in the form of a bar chart and indicates the influence of the individual factors on the total quantity in percent. The individual factors are shown in order of importance from left to right. Their cumulative calculation always results in the value of 100%.

Use/Benefit

The Pareto Chart is used to visualise, narrow down and compare different data groups in a simple way. One look is enough to see which of the different data groups has the strongest impact on the issue and should be analysed in depth accordingly.

In improvement management, the Pareto Chart is often used to illustrate the causes of existing problems, such as the mapping of error frequencies in a workflow. Thanks to this tool, the main causes can be identified quickly and a targeted limitation to and focus on a few decisive causes is made possible.

Description

The Pareto Chart is well suited for use in a workshop with the employees involved. In the first part, the causes and their weighting are worked out. In the second part, the actual diagram is created.

Part 1: Development of Causes and Weighting

The following procedure is used to work out the causes and their weighting:

1. The first step in the joint workshop is to formulate the problem as precisely as possible. It is important that all participants have the same understanding of the existing problem.
2. Next, the possible causes are collected, written on slips of paper, and pinned to a board. The brainstorming method is very suitable for this.
3. The collected causes are discussed together in the team and formulated in detail. At the same time, similar causes are grouped together into cause groups.
4. In order to compare the causes, they must be evaluated uniformly in the next step. For this purpose, a suitable measurement parameter is determined. This can be, for example, quantity, frequency or costs.
5. In the next step, the measurement data for the assessment must be determined. If no data are available yet, they must be determined, for example, through interviews, observations, or the use of tally sheets.
6. The data collected on the individual causes are compiled in a table. In a separate column, the percentage of the total value is calculated for each cause and sorted in descending order. This table is the basis for creating the Pareto Chart.

Note: Steps one to three can also be done with the help of an Ishikawa Diagram. This enables a targeted procedure to determine the causes. See the description of the Ishikawa Diagram in Sect. 4.1.7.

Part 2: Creating the Pareto Chart

The manual creation of a Pareto Chart is relatively time-consuming. Thanks to preconfigured graphics, however, it is very easy to create one quickly in common software programmes. For this, the following steps are necessary:

1. The table resulting from the recording and evaluation of the causes is inserted into the corresponding programme.
2. The corresponding diagram type is selected in the programme. The subsequent creation of the graph takes place automatically. If the Pareto Chart is not explicitly available for selection, a simple bar chart can also be used.
3. The completed Pareto Chart is then analysed in the team and the causes which are to be eliminated with targeted measures are determined. As a general rule, the causes with the largest percentage are to be prioritised.

Example

As a basis for the creation of a Pareto Chart, we use the example with the question about the sub-optimal stock of goods in the grocery shop. See the example of the Ishikawa Diagram (Sect. 4.1.7). After recording the various causes of stock issues, the store manager keeps a tally for a month to determine the frequency of each cause. The resulting Pareto Chart is shown in Fig. 4.14.

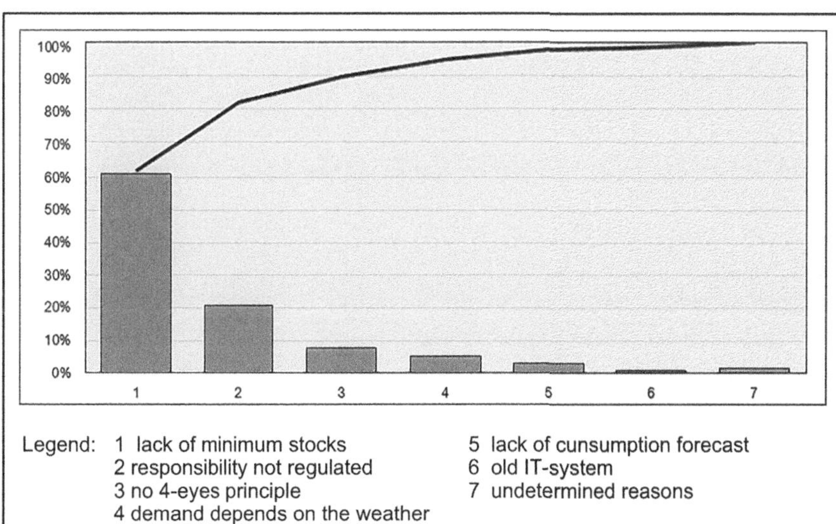

Fig. 4.14 Pareto Chart

The result shows that the two causes 'lack of minimum stocks' and 'responsibility not regulated' are responsible for 80% of the missing stocks.

Tips and tricks

1. It makes sense to group small non-essential factors in the category 'undetermined reasons'. However, it is important to ensure that this category does not become too large.
2. Use existing knowledge and facts. When creating the Pareto Chart, the results of a previously created Ishikawa Diagram can help.
3. Estimates of the database are often too inaccurate. Therefore, determine the data basis as precisely as possible, for example, by using a tally sheet.

4.1.10 Utility-Value Analysis

The Utility-Value Analysis is suitable for presenting various alternative courses of action. In particular, this tool supports the comparison of alternatives for which no easily quantifiable criteria are available. Accordingly, the Utility-Value Analysis is an excellent tool for making a decision when there are several options to choose from.

Use/Benefit

The Utility-Value Analysis is used as an aid when there are various alternative courses of action and it is difficult to decide on one of the variants available for selection. The individual alternatives are made comparable with jointly defined criteria, which are subsequently evaluated. The transparent derivation aids in choosing the better alternative and displays its effect in relation to the selected evaluation criteria at the same time.

Description

The following procedure is used to prepare the Utility-Value Analysis:

Preparation

In order to be able to quickly start evaluating the individual alternative courses of action in the joint workshop, the grid for the Utility-Value Analysis must first be drawn up. To do this, proceed as follows:

1. First, the grid is drawn on a large brown paper. It is important to ensure that there are enough columns for the alternatives to be assessed and enough rows for the necessary assessment criteria. An example of the structure of the grid is shown in Fig. 4.15.
2. Then the individual alternative courses of action available for selection are entered in the columns. These different alternatives usually originate from a previous improvement workshop. It is important to note that only alternative courses of action that fulfil the specified objectives may be listed.
3. To be able to work on it together, the finished grid is hung on a wall in a clearly visible position.

Create Rating

The evaluation of the individual alternative courses of action is done together with the employees involved. Ideally, it should be ensured that the group of participants comprises the same people as during the development of the alternatives available for selection. Otherwise, there is a risk that instead of evaluating the alternative courses of action, new options will be sought.

1. At the beginning, the individual evaluation criteria are worked out together in the group and entered in the empty rows of the grid. These criteria can often be derived from the fact sheet of the improvement project.

criterion	weighting in %	mobile phone with camera		compact camera		system camera		SLR camera	
		evaluation	benefit	evaluation	benefit	evaluation	benefit	evaluation	benefit
handling	25%	8	2.00	8	2.00	4	1.00	3	0.75
photo quality	25%	3	0.75	5	1.25	9	2.25	9	2.25
size of the camera	10%	9	0.90	6	0.60	4	0.40	1	0.10
weight	5%	9	0.45	7	0.35	5	0.25	3	0.15
price	15%	10	1.50	6	0.90	3	0.45	3	0.45
availability	20%	10	2.00	4	0.80	4	0.80	4	0.80
utility	100%	7.60		5.90		5.15		4.50	
ranking list		1		2		3		4	

Fig. 4.15 Utility-Value Analysis

2. Not all criteria are equally decisive for the evaluation. This aspect is considered by weighting the individual criteria in the next step. This can be done, for example, as follows: Each participant performs an individual weighting. Then the average is entered into the grid as a parameter. The sum of the individual weightings is equal to a total of 100%.
3. Next, the evaluation is carried out. This is done by awarding points to every alternative for each criterion. Ten is the highest possible number.
4. After the completed grading, the utility value of the individual alternative courses of action is calculated. Again, points are awarded to every alternative for each criterion. The sum of all benefits equals the utility value per alternative course of action.
5. Now the utility values for all alternatives are known and can be compared with each other. The alternative course of action with the highest utility value obtains the highest ranking and is to be favoured.

Example

An event organiser used to hire a professional photographer to take promotional pictures of his events for publication on the Internet and in social media. In order to reduce the resulting costs, they decide to have the required pictures taken by their employees instead. For this reason, they want to look into the acquisition of a suitable camera. Together with their employees, they prepare a Utility-Value Analysis to figure out the various options. The result of the evaluation is shown in Fig. 4.15.

The result of the Utility-Value Analysis shows that the option of taking photos with one's own mobile phone clearly comes out on top. The quality is certainly sufficient for use on social media, and if one considers the simple handling and constant availability, this alternative is clearly the best. Also, this is the most cost-effective option, as no new camera has to be purchased.

Tips and Tricks

1. It is helpful to proceed row by row in the assessment. This means that each alternative course of action is evaluated for one particular evaluation criterion before moving on to the next evaluation criterion. This makes it possible to immediately assess whether the scoring per criterion is consistent across the alternative courses of action.
2. When entering the individual scores, the resulting score should not be calculated directly. Indeed, this could lead to hasty comparisons and a possible distortion of the results. Instead, I always write down the individual scores on a separate board first and only transfer them to the grid at the very end in order to calculate the result afterwards.
3. If the implementation costs are not included in the evaluation criteria, it can still make sense to take them into account when cost-intensive alternatives are being considered. To do this, the calculated utility value is divided by the implementation costs. The result is the utility value per monetary unit.
4. In situations where the weighting and evaluation are difficult and ambiguous, an alternative evaluation can be performed by adjusting the weighting of the criteria. Hence it can be deduced how stable the determined result is and under which circumstances it changes.

4.1.11 Cost-Benefit Analysis

The Cost-Benefit Analysis is used to compare different potential solutions with regard to the expected implementation cost and the resulting benefit. Thanks to the graphic representation, the cost-benefit ratio is clearly visible. In addition, the absolute benefit of the individual potential solutions can be read off.

Use/Benefit

The Cost-Benefit Analysis is used when different potential solutions are available for selection. With this tool, the different solutions are assessed in terms of their effectiveness and displayed graphically.

The main challenge in creating a Cost-Benefit Analysis is to determine the expected costs as precisely as possible and to judge the benefits. In order to obtain a result that is as objective as possible, a joint assessment with the staff concerned in the form of a workshop is suitable.

Description

The following procedure is used to create a Cost-Benefit Analysis:

Preparation

1. As a first step, the *x*- and *y*-axes are drawn on a brown paper and pinned to the wall. The vertical axis represents the 'benefit' and the horizontal axis the 'cost' of each solution.
2. Next, the diagram area is divided into three segments (see Fig. 4.16). The description of the segments is as follows: Segment 1: 'Pursue idea'; Segment 2:

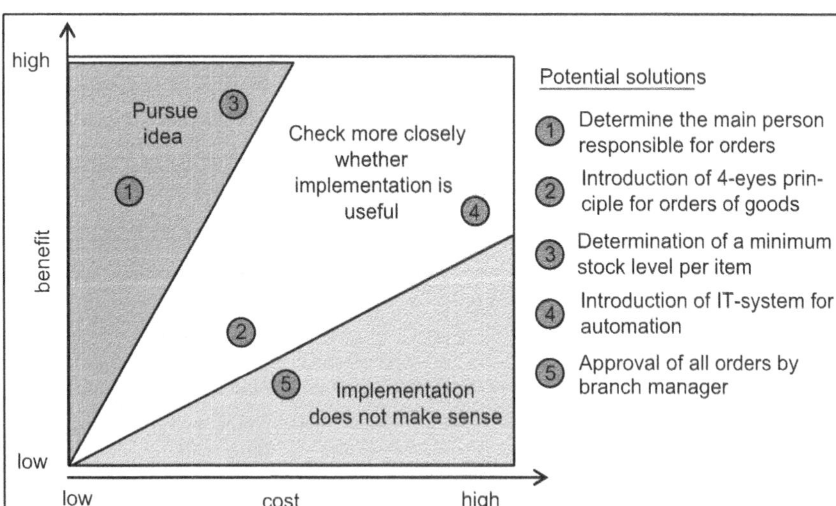

Fig. 4.16 Cost-Benefit Analysis

'Check more closely whether implementation makes sense'; Segment 3: 'Implementation not useful'.

3. The solutions to be assessed, including their detailed description, are hung separately next to the prepared grid. These can be the result of an earlier improvement workshop.

Create the Cost-Benefit Analysis

After the preparation of the grid, the assessment and recording of the individual potential solutions can begin. This is done together with the staff involved according to the following steps:

1. First, the terms 'cost' and 'benefit' need to be clearly defined in the team. It must be clear to everyone what is covered by these two terms.
2. Subsequently, the costs and benefits for each solution to be assessed are determined in detail. It is important to include both the monetary and non-monetary part.
3. A point is now plotted on the graph for each potential solution. This point is located at the intersection of the determined cost and benefit.
4. The result is then analysed together in the team. The following principle applies to the individual segments of the graph:
   - *Segment 1:* All potential solutions that fall into this part of the graph have a higher benefit compared to the cost. These solutions should therefore be pursued and implemented.
   - *Segment 2:* Cost and benefit of the potential solutions in this part of the graph roughly balance each other out. Therefore, it is not possible to clearly determine whether an implementation would make sense. These potential solutions are to be examined in more detail in a further step.
   - *Segment 3:* The potential solutions in this part of the graph have a lower benefit compared to the cost. Therefore, these solutions should not be pursued further.

Example

As a basis for the creation of the Cost-Benefit Analysis, we use the example with the question about the sub-optimal stock of goods in the grocery shop. See the examples of the Ishikawa Diagram (Sect. 4.1.7) and the Pareto Chart (Sect. 4.1.9).

Based on these previous evaluations, the branch manager defined various improvement options together with his employees. The following potential solutions were derived:

1. A main person responsible for ordering goods shall be determined. This person is responsible for all orders.
2. The four-eyes principle should apply to all orders of goods. This means that all orders placed are checked by a second employee before they are initiated.

3. A minimum stock level is set for each item. Every evening, it should be checked whether the stock level has fallen below this minimum. If this is the case, an order is initiated.
4. A powerful IT-system is to partially automate the ordering process and strongly assist the employees in ordering.
5. All orders of goods are submitted daily to the branch manager for approval.

These five potential solutions are assessed together in the team in terms of cost and benefit, and then entered accordingly in the Cost-Benefit Analysis. The result is shown in Fig. 4.16.

Based on these findings, potential solutions ‘1’ and ‘3’ should be implemented as quickly as possible. For solutions ‘2’ and ‘4’, it must be reconsidered whether implementation makes sense. The implementation of solution ‘5’ should be abandoned due to the high cost involved.

Tips and Tricks

1. In my experience, the Cost-Benefit Analysis provides a good first overview of the effectiveness of the various solutions. However, in very few cases does it replace a detailed analysis.

4.1.12 Brainstorming

Brainstorming is a widely used method for generating common ideas in groups. The aim is to use the creativity of the participants and to find unconventional solutions. A facilitator ensures a structured procedure and makes sure that all participants can contribute their experience and knowledge.

Brainstorming is the best-known and most widely used creative technique and is designed to promote inventive thinking among participants. It can generate helpful ideas and viable solutions in a short time.

Use/Benefit

Brainstorming is used to involve stakeholders in the solution-finding process and to develop common ideas while doing so. In improvement management, the focus is on generating suggestions for solutions to existing problems and increasing efficiency. Brainstorming is often used in conjunction with other tools or as part of an improvement workshop.

Description

Not a lot of preparation is necessary to conduct a brainstorming session. However, circumspect facilitation of the brainstorming is crucial for a positive output, as well as for generating many useful ideas. The procedure is as follows:

1. As an introduction to brainstorming, the facilitator briefly introduces the method. It is important that the applicable rules are defined and posted on the wall so that they are clearly visible. The rules include the following points in particular:
   - Allow all parties to speak and listen to them.
   - Make every suggestion count.
   - Consider and write down all contributions.
   - No counterproductive statements.
   - Do not comment on and rate each other's contributions.
   - No content-related discussion and no explanations.
   - The more daring and imaginative the contribution, the better.
2. Next, the facilitator explains the issue to be addressed. This can, for example, stem from the fact sheet of the improvement project or from an earlier Actual-Condition Analysis. If no issue was predetermined, it should be discussed and defined together in the team. It is important that all participants understand the issue correctly.
3. At the start of the brainstorming phase, the facilitator announces the time frame. Depending on the complexity of the topic, a duration of 10–15 min is recommended.
4. In the brainstorming phase, the participants express their ideas on the given issue. All contributions are recorded by the facilitator on individual pieces of paper and pinned onto a flipchart in an unsorted order.
5. After the ideas have been collected, the contributions noted on the flipchart are briefly discussed in the group to ensure a general understanding. At the same

time, it is checked whether the individual contributions can be condensed into key topics.
6. Depending on the results of the first round, it may be useful to add a second brainstorming phase to generate further suggestions for improvement. It is possible that more in-depth or new approaches will emerge from ideas already collected.

Variants of Brainstorming

Based on the classic brainstorming method, other interesting variants for generating ideas in groups have been developed in recent years. Brainwriting or Anti-Brainstorming are such variants.

Brainwriting

Brainwriting is a variant of classic brainstorming. Instead of expressing ideas verbally, they are put in writing. Brainwriting is used to develop ideas together in a quiet atmosphere. Shy participants in particular can develop their ideas better in this way than in classic brainstorming. Another advantage of brainwriting is that not all participants have to be in the same room. Instead of writing on a piece of paper, the idea for a solution can be written in an e-mail and then passed on to the next participant.

Brainwriting differs from the classic variant in the following points:

1. Each participant writes down an idea for a solution to the defined issue on a piece of paper (slip of paper, sticky note).
2. The sheets are passed on to the next participant simultaneously.
3. Everyone first examines the idea they have received. Then they develop it further, building on it or creating a completely new idea.
4. The sheets are passed on to the next participant simultaneously and worked on again.
5. After the agreed time has elapsed, all sheets are collected by the facilitator and pinned to a wall.
6. Finally, the ideas are discussed and evaluated together with the participants. If necessary, they will be grouped into main topics.

As a variation, 6-3-5 Brainwriting can be used. Here, 6 people each write down 3 ideas in 5 min and pass them on.

Reverse Brainstorming

Reverse brainstorming is used to remove blockages during the generation of ideas. The process is the same as in classic brainstorming. However, the first step is not to find solutions to an issue. Instead, the aim is to collect ideas that make the existing situation even worse. The procedure is as follows:

1. The participants name ideas for making the current situation worse. For example, for the question 'how to make the tracking of open customer invoices in the company worse', this may look like the following:
   - *Idea for deterioration:* Reconciliation meetings between departments are abolished altogether. The tracking of open invoices is done independently in the individual departments.
2. These ideas are written on cards by the facilitator in the same way as in classic brainstorming and hung on the board. Red cards are used to clearly mark the ideas for deterioration.
3. After the collection of ideas has been completed, they are discussed together and, if it makes sense, grouped into main topics.
4. In the next step, solutions are sought together to transform the collected ideas for deterioration into suggestions for improvement. For the example mentioned, this could be:
   - *Suggestion for improvement: The introduction of a central office to monitor all open customer invoices. This suggestion for improvement is now written on a green card and hung next to the red card with the idea for deterioration.*

Tips and Tricks

1. Choose the variant of brainstorming based on the group of participants and the issue at hand. Depending on the initial situation, the various techniques are of different suitability.
2. It is crucial that the established rules are consistently adhered to. It is precisely the commenting on the ideas of other contributors and the use of killer phrases that paralyses creativity in the group and thus the further generation of ideas.

4.1.13 Burn Down Chart

With the help of the Burn Down Chart, the progress of projects can be measured and visually mapped. The tool is an important part of management in agile projects such as Scrum projects. However, there is no reason why the Burn Down Chart cannot be used in other projects as well.

Use/Benefit

The Burn Down Chart is used to monitor the progress of a project that is being implemented. It assists in the early detection of delays compared to the schedule. This enables the rapid initiation of appropriate measures when delays occur.

The chart is created by displaying the remaining workload until the completion of the project in relation to the remaining time until the planned end of the project. This allows for a current and precise statement on the progress of the project. In addition, it becomes apparent by when the remaining work will be completed and whether the planned completion date can be met.

Description

The Burn Down Chart is a supportive working tool that is constantly updated and regularly reviewed and discussed within the implementation team and in the project meeting. It is to be displayed clearly visible and accessible for all staff involved in the implementation. The Burn Down Chart is structured as follows (see also Fig. 4.17):

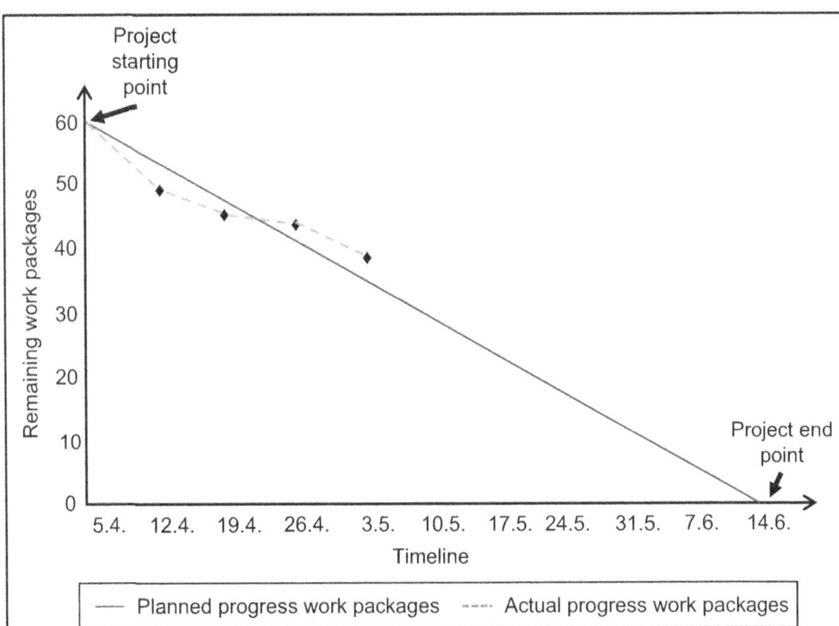

Fig. 4.17 Burn Down Chart

- *Horizontal axis:* Timeline of the project until the planned end of the project. This can be measured in working days or calendar weeks, for example.
- *Vertical axis:* Remaining workload until completion of the project. This can be the estimated remaining effort in working days or the number of work packages to be completed. It should be noted that when using work packages as estimates, they must have approximately the same duration.
- *Project start point:* Represents the beginning of the project and corresponds to the sum of the total work hours or work packages to be carried out during the duration of the project.
- *Project end point:* Represents the planned end of the project. At this point, all work packages should have been completed.
- *Line Planned Progress Work Packages:* It connects the project start point and the project end point in the normal course of the project and represents the planned progress of the project. Assuming the same number of resources are available throughout the project, this is a straight line from the start point to the end point.
- *Line Actual Progress Work Packages:* This line shows the course of the effectively completed hours or work packages. To determine it, the work packages completed are subtracted from the remaining work packages and plotted on the graph. The individual points are then connected with a line. The deviation from the planned progress line shows whether the project is on schedule.

The chart is to be interpreted as follows:

- The line 'actual progress of work packages' is above the line 'planned progress of work packages'. In this case, more work packages remain than planned. Thus, the project is behind schedule.
- The line 'actual progress of work packages' is below the line 'planned progress of work packages'. In this case, fewer work packages remain than planned. Thus, the project is ahead of schedule.

Example

A company is planning to introduce a new software for more efficient warehouse management. The implementation is carried out in collaboration with the manufacturer of the software and should be completed by 14 June.

In order to continuously track and effectively control the progress of the project, all activities necessary for implementation were divided into 60 work packages of approximately equal size. These work packages each correspond to a self-contained sub-product, which can be tested and accepted by the end user after completion. Currently, 20 work packages have already been completed. The progress of the project is continuously recorded in a Burn Down Chart and discussed with all participants in weekly project meetings. The current status of the project is shown in Fig. 4.17.

The Burn Down Chart shows that the project initially started out very well and the first work packages were completed faster than planned. In the meantime, however, the completion of the work packages is behind schedule and additional effort is needed to reach the planned project end point.

Tips and Tricks

1. If there are large fluctuations in the available resources, it makes sense to include this in the planning. As a result, the line ‘planned progress work packages’ may no longer be linear.
2. Instead of the tasks, the decisive milestones can also be drawn on the vertical axis. This is particularly helpful if no reliable estimate of the detailed workload can be made.
3. The chart is only useful if it is continuously updated and displayed in a way that is clearly visible and accessible to the whole team.

4.1.14 Implementation Plan

The Implementation Plan is used to organise the implementation of the measures decided in the improvement project. In the process, the respective responsibilities as well as the timelines are defined for all activities. The deadlines set also serve as a basis for monitoring the implementation. The Implementation Plan is also referred to as the Action Plan or Realisation Plan. In the Kaizen method, it is known as the 'Kaizen Newspaper'.

Use/Benefit

At the end of an improvement project, the optimisations already implemented are documented and applied in daily operations. At the same time, all measures still to be implemented are followed up with the Implementation Plan. This plan serves as a guideline and checklist for the activities that still need to be completed and thus ensures that the outstanding measures are consistently addressed and implemented.

Description

The following procedure is used for the preparation of the Implementation Plan:

Preparation

1. The first step is to create an empty grid for recording the individual activities. This is structured as follows (see also Fig. 4.18):
   - *Columns:* In the individual columns, the titles 'Task', 'Responsible', 'Implementation period' (as a time bar), 'Deadline' and 'Comments' are to be entered.
   - *Lines:* The lines are intended for recording the individual activities. For better readability, it makes sense to divide them into thematic blocks.
2. If it is to be used in a workshop, the grid is ideally drawn on a large sheet of paper. This makes it easier to fill it in together with the participants. The paper sheet can be taken away after the workshop for documentation.
3. All available documents from the current improvement project are to be hung on the wall next to the paper sheet in a clearly visible place. These serve as input for the definition of the individual activities.

Creation

The prepared grid is completed together with the employees concerned. Otherwise, the necessary support and knowledge will be lacking when implementing the measures and applying them in day-to-day operations.

1. The first question that needs to be answered is what has to be in place at the end of the implementation. This can be deduced from the objective and the developed findings of the improvement project.
2. Next, set a deadline for the completion of each activity. Rapid implementation is clearly preferable. Otherwise, there is a risk that the optimisations will not be implemented at all.

Task	Respon-sible	Implementation period								Dead-line	Comments
		week 1	week 2	week 3	week 4	week 5	week 6	week 7	week 8		
Creation of the new expense regulations											
Creation of new and uniform regulations	Tim	■	■							12.1.	
Approval by the Executive Board	Tim			■						21.1.	
Publication of the new regulations	John					■				4.2.	
Design of a uniform expense form											
Creation of a uniform expense form	Brian			■	■					28.1.	
Publication of the expense form	John					■				4.2.	
Communicate the results and measures of the workshop to management and staff											
Communication of the re-sults to the management	Oliver	■								7.1.	
Communication via branch managers	John and branch managers					■				4.2.	Guide for branch managers
Publication in the internal newsletter	John					■				4.2.	
Conduct a review of the improvement workshop											
Perform review	Oliver								■	23.2.	
Create final report	Oliver								■	25.2.	

Fig. 4.18 Implementation Plan

3. In the next step, concrete work packages are to be put together from the solution approaches developed in the joint improvement workshops.
4. For each work package, corresponding detailed measures are to be decided. It is very important to define a person responsible for the implementation of each activity. In addition, each activity must be given a deadline. All this information must be entered into the Implementation Plan.
5. Finally, a date should be set for the review of the improvement project and its effect.

Example

A tour operator runs sales outlets in different cities. There, the employees' expenses have been accounted for in very different ways up until now. Neither clear instructions nor uniform and binding expense forms exist. In some cases, expenses are paid together with wages, or via the local cash registers. Within the framework of an improvement project, various optimisations are decided upon and recorded in the Implementation Plan according to Fig. 4.18.

Tips and Tricks

1. The aim should be to implement as many of the optimisations as possible while the improvement project is still being worked on. Only activities that could not already be implemented during the improvement project should be included in the Implementation Plan.
2. Communication to all stakeholders is crucial for the successful implementation of the improvement measures. Therefore, the communication of the results from the improvement project as well as the adopted measures is a central point in the Implementation Plan.
3. Employees who were also involved in the development of the measures and the preparation of the Implementation Plan should be chosen as those responsible for implementation.
4. From my own personal experience, I recommend not writing directly into the grid of the Implementation Plan, but working with self-adhesive notes. This makes it possible to easily adjust or move points that have already been recorded.

4.1.15 Documentation of Improvement Projects

This is less of a tool and more of a guideline for creating documentation of completed improvement projects. A clear and goal-oriented compilation of the most important findings, measures and agreed adjustments is a central element for the consistent implementation and sustainable effect of improvement projects.

The documentation is not just created at the end of the improvement project, but it is continuously added to at each stage of the process. This means that the documentation is complete immediately after the conclusion of the project and can be distributed quickly to the participants and interested stakeholders. Only its prompt preparation and communication will bring the desired benefits. Or are you interested in a final report that appears weeks after a project has been concluded?

Use/Benefit

The documentation of an improvement project provides the basis for communicating the findings and for tracking the decisions made. Specifically, documentation is needed for the following purposes, among others:

- *Communication basis:* Serves as a basis for communicating the findings of the improvement project to the staff and all stakeholders.
- *Presentation to management:* The One Pager is used to communicate the results to the management.
- *Tracking of implementation:* The Implementation Plan is part of the documentation and is used to monitor the implementation.
- *Basis for review:* The documentation serves as the basis for the review of the improvement project. This review takes place a few weeks after completion.
- *Basis for further improvement projects:* Last but not least, the documentation serves as a guide for similar projects and for knowledge transfer.

Description

The documentation is continuously supplemented while the improvement project is being worked on and thus serves as a basis for the following processing steps. The simplest and most efficient way to realise the documentation is with photos of the tools and documents developed. The structure of the documentation depends very much on the processing procedure. At least, the following contents must be included:

- *Management summary (one pager):* Summary of the results achieved based on the initial situation and the goals set on the fact sheet.
- *Fact Sheet:* As an introduction, the approved fact sheet of the improvement project is displayed in the documentation.
- *Procedure:* This item shows the procedure for solving the problem. This includes, among other things, a compilation of the tools used, and the insights gained from them.
- *Measures taken:* The measures taken to improve the workflow are described here.

- *Benefit:* Under this item, the benefits (monetary and non-monetary) of the optimisations are presented. It also shows whether the goals set have been achieved.
- *Sustainability of the optimisation:* This shows how the future monitoring of the workflow is ensured.
- *Lessons learned from the improvement project:* This item describes what contributed to the success and what hindered the processing.

It is crucial that not only detailed documentation is produced, but that the findings are also communicated accordingly. The following formats are particularly suitable for communication:

- *Final presentation by the team working on the project:* Offers another good opportunity to reflect on the results achieved and serves as an information platform for all interested stakeholders.
- *Present findings to the management:* Using the One Pager, the results are presented to the divisional and executive management.
- *Documentation in written form:* The documentation of the improvement project is made available to all interested stakeholders via the intranet. In addition, the findings are presented in internal newsletters, for instance.

And especially important: Do not forget to celebrate the successes achieved with everyone involved!

Example

Figure 4.19 shows a possible depiction of a One Pager. It is important that the connection between the initial situation and the objective is shown. This way it is quickly visible whether the improvement project is successful or not.

Tips and Tricks

1. The documentation should be kept up to date on an ongoing basis. This simplifies the completion of the project and serves as continuous interim documentation at the same time.
2. Achievements and optimisations from completed improvement projects should be marketed accordingly. This helps to further anchor improvement management in the corporation and supports new projects.
3. The documentation for the completion of the improvement project should always be prepared according to the same specifications and standards. This simplifies its creation and leads to a recognition effect for the reader.

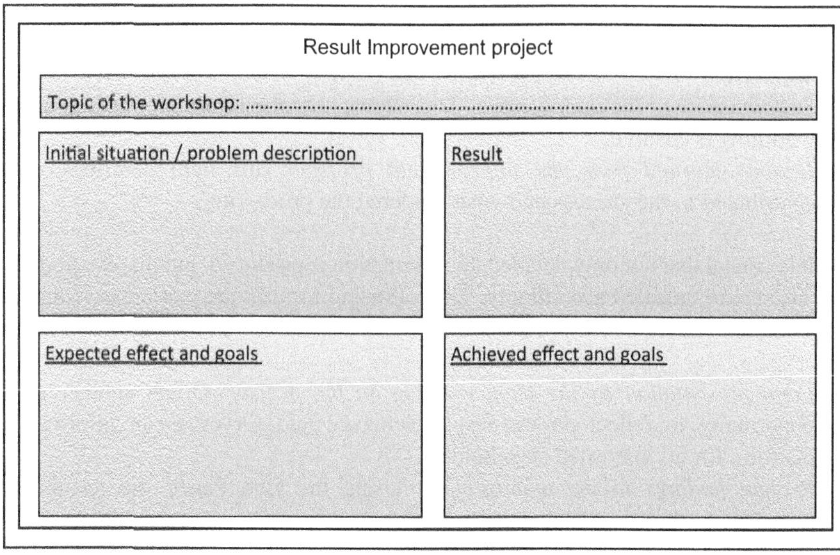

Fig. 4.19 Summary of improvement projects (One Pager)

4.2 The Maturity Model

A regular review of the status of processes is crucial for their efficient and sustainable further development. The Maturity Model is a tried and tested tool for this purpose, which ensures a structured procedure with comparable results. Thanks to the measurement of maturity, existing weaknesses in the workflows are revealed and necessary process improvements are identified. Over time, different variants of the Maturity Model have become established, depending on the area of application and environment. While these are largely identical in procedure, they differ in the assessment criteria applied. The most common Maturity Models include:

- *CMMI (Capability Maturity Model Integration):* The origin of this model goes back to IBM's Maturity Model for software development. In the meantime, CMMI models have been developed for different applications, such as assessment in the service sector.
- *Maturity Model ISO 9004:2009:* The ISO 9004:2009 standard recommends carrying out a maturity assessment and presents a corresponding model. This is a relatively simple, generally applicable model that can be used for the assessment of processes.
- *BPMM (Business Process Maturity Model):* This is a model that was developed specifically for the assessment of business processes in industrial companies. This model has a high level of detail and is therefore complex to apply.

A detailed description of the most important Maturity Models can be found in Schmelzer and Sesselmann (2013).

The Maturity Model can be used in many different ways. In addition to the assessment of individual work processes, it is also suitable for a standardised assessment of entire process systems as well as for determining the maturity of organisational units such as individual teams or departments. The Maturity Model also provides an important basis for company-wide comparisons in regard to benchmarks.

4.2.1 Use/Benefit

The Maturity Model is used within the framework of improvement management to regularly determine the maturity of work processes. This is done by dividing the processes to be evaluated into different maturity levels as part of an assessment. This allows them to be compared and rated. A high level of maturity means that the prerequisites for high effectiveness and efficiency are met.

In addition to the possibility of comparing different workflows, the results from the Maturity Model can provide important insights into the development of the individual workflows over time. For this purpose, the current assessment of a process is compared with previous assessments of the same process.

In order to increase the significance of the maturity measurement, the measurement is broken down into different sub-areas. When assessing a workflow in the office sector, for example, these can be the following sub-areas:

- *Process definition:* Assesses the correct definition of the workflow, the roles involved, the assignment of activities to these roles and the responsibilities.
- *Process scheduling:* Assesses how the timing of the workflow is managed and how much idle time there is.
- *Process control:* Here, it is assessed how the processes are controlled and which measurements and key figures are used for this purpose.
- *Process optimisation:* How improvement activities are selected, implemented, and sustainably anchored is assessed.
- *Process standardisation:* This sub-area assesses the standardisation of work processes that has been achieved.

Based on the assessment carried out, it can be easily determined in which work processes and in which sub-areas the greatest need for action exists. In addition, the information gained from the process assessments provides important inputs to the individual fields of action.

Figure 4.20 shows possible evaluation criteria for assessing maturity in the sub-area of process standardisation. Uniform assessment criteria are crucial to ensure a comparable assessment of the different work processes.

4.2.2 Procedure

The generation of valid and meaningful results in maturity measurement depends heavily on conscientious preparation and execution. Only if it is performed uniformly and in a clearly defined way, a meaningful comparison between the different work processes to be assessed becomes possible. Moreover, reliable comparisons with previous measurements are only feasible if the same procedure is followed. The maturity level is assessed in interviews with the employees involved in the process. These interviews are called process assessments.

Detailed preparation is particularly important when conducting the maturity measurement for the first time. The choice of the model to be used and the definition of the exact procedure strongly determine the future direction. In detail, the procedure for measuring the maturity level is as follows:

Preparatory Steps When Carrying Out a Maturity Measurement for the First Time

1. When measuring the maturity level of workflows for the first time, it is important to determine the exact purpose of the measurement and the goals pursued with it beforehand. This provides the basis for choosing the right Maturity Model and is the foundation for the entire implementation.
2. Based on the defined purpose and goals, the appropriate Maturity Model is then selected. There are many different models with various characteristics and

Process standardisation			
	Level 0 No standardisation available	**Level 1** Standardisation has been addressed	**Level 2** Standardisation is introduced
	- There is no standardised procedure. - Each employee carries out the activities at their own discretion. - There are no checklists or work instructions.	- Individual activities with-in the workflow are stan-dardised. However, these are the exception. - The first simple checklists and instructions for cer-tain activities exist. How-ever, these are not used.	- All activities within the workflow are standardised. - The documentation of in-dividual activities is still incomplete and not yet known to all staff. - The employees do not yet consistently apply the es-tablished standards. - Training on the standards does not yet exist.
	Level 3 Standards are known to all employees	**Level 4** Standardisation is lived	**Level 5** Standardisation is lived and further developed
	- The standards are de-fined, communicated and trained. - All activities are docu-mented. However, some of the documents are not up to date. - The employees only partially apply the set standards and do not use the work instructions consistently.	- Standardisation is visible everywhere. - The standards are up to date and available when needed. - Staff are trained in the standards and under-stand why and where they are used.	- The standards set are regularly updated and furt-her developed. - The standards are always up-to-date and available online at any time. - There is a standardised process for incorporating adjustments to the stan-dards into process mana-gement. - All employees work consi-stently according to stan-dardised specifications.

Fig. 4.20 Evaluation criteria for assessing maturity in the sub-area of process standardisation

different emphases. Depending on the purpose, goals and area of application, the specific models can be more or less suitable.

3. Before the maturity assessment can begin, the chosen model is adapted to the particular circumstances of the company. This includes specifying the sub-areas for which the maturity level is to be determined, as well as additions or reformulations of assessment questions, if necessary. It should be noted that if too many changes are made to the model, a comparison with other companies may become more difficult and less meaningful.

Steps in the Recurring Implementation of the Maturity Measurement

1. If maturity measurements have already been carried out in the past, it is sufficient to check the defined purpose and the pursued goals for their current validity and to adjust them slightly if necessary.
2. Next, the workflows to be included in the maturity assessment are selected. An assessment can be made of all existing workflows or only of a specific part.

3. For each selected workflow, the persons who will be involved in the assessments must be determined. Normally, these are the most important persons involved in the process, who tend to be the persons responsible for the process as well.
4. Once it is known which work processes are to be examined, it is determined how many assessors are needed for this. These are to be selected and prepared for their task accordingly. For the comparability of the results, it is crucial that when several assessors are used, they carry out a uniform assessment. To ensure this, appropriate training must be provided and detailed checklists drawn up.
5. Before the start of the process assessments, it is important that those involved are well informed about the planned survey. To promote acceptance and support, it is essential that the purpose, the goals and the procedure are explained in detail.
6. The next step is to carry out the process assessments. This takes one to two hours per workflow, depending on its complexity and the number of employees involved. It is important that all answers received, and the classifications therefrom derived are immediately entered into the grid provided.
7. The evaluations as well as the resulting graphs should only be created and analysed after the process assessment has been completed. These can be, for example, comparisons between the different workflows surveyed, comparisons with previous measurements or comparisons with other companies. Although the evaluations and graphs are continuously updated when they are entered into the tool, they should not be shown and discussed during the process assessment, as this could influence and distort the further answers.
8. The evaluations and graphs are discussed in separate meetings with those involved in the respective work processes. In addition, based on the results, the main fields of action for targeted improvements are jointly determined. The derivation and definition of concrete improvement measures are the task of those responsible for the process.
9. At the end of the maturity measurement, a detailed final report is prepared. This contains the individual assessments, the graphical evaluations and the defined fields of action per workflow. An aggregated version is sent to the management for approval and to determine the next steps.
10. The final step is the internal communication of the results and further measures decided upon. Here, it is important for the acceptance and further anchoring of improvement management in the company that this communication comes directly from the management and involves all employees. This also applies if the management was not directly involved in the maturity measurement.

4.2.3 Result

The result of a maturity measurement is best presented in a Spider Chart. This simple graphical evaluation quickly and clearly presents the results of the analysed work processes by breaking them down into the selected sub-areas. In particular, the Spider Chart is a good way of making comparisons with previous measurements.

Mapping results using a Spider Chart is an integral part of the most common maturity measurement models. It can easily be created in the common calculation tools. Figure 4.21 shows an example of a graphical evaluation using a Spider Chart.

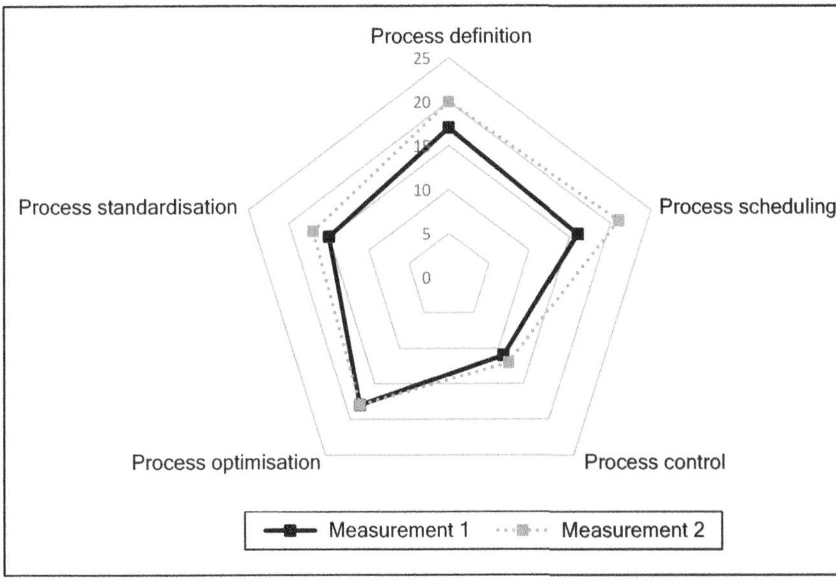

Fig. 4.21 Result of maturity measurement

4.3 Practical Experience of an Expert with the Maturity Model

The correct application of the model in practice and the avoidance of various stumbling blocks are crucial for a reliable and meaningful result of the maturity measurement. Kateryna Brönnimann knows this from her own personal experience, as she was involved in the development and testing of a new Maturity Model at the Swiss Federal Railways (SBB) and wrote her master's thesis on this topic.

Kateryna Brönnimann completed a part-time master's degree in Business Administration at the Bern University of Applied Sciences with a specialisation in corporate and business development. Prior to that, she completed a bachelor's and master's degree in Economics and Entrepreneurship with a specialisation in Finance in Ukraine. She currently works for the Swiss Federal Railways as a corporate controller in the investment field. She is responsible for ensuring second level support in the field of investment accounting (SAP modules PS, PS+, BI and PPM) as well as for optimising and further developing the financial management of investment accounting and the associated systems.

In the following interview, Kateryna Brönnimann talks about her experiences in designing the Maturity Model at the Swiss Federal Railways.

Hello Kateryna, How Did You First Come into Contact with the Maturity Model?

I would like to begin with my personal start at SBB. I started my career with a university internship in the field of Operating. Operating is the production and maintenance sector of SBB's passenger services and is responsible for the operation and maintenance of trains. I was able to actively get to know the Kaizen philosophy. I was surrounded by Kaizen everywhere. Especially in production, I had the chance to see how Kaizen was applied in the various maintenance facilities. I found this extremely exciting. In the office sector, operating had also made a lot of progress. You could feel that the philosophy was understood and lived. But I asked myself one question: What happens after the introduction of the Kaizen philosophy? How do you check whether the concept works have an effect on the whole organisation?

I learnt that audits are conducted in different areas for this purpose. For example, in the field of sales, services and marketing, which is mostly concerned with administrative activities, the Kaizen audit form was used as the main tool. It was introduced in 2010 and no longer offered the desired added value these days, as the same detailed questions were asked over and over again and new focal points could only be set to a limited extent. Additionally, working with the audit form has become a routine process in the meantime and offered practically no room for deviations. Also, the cost/benefit ratio with the audit form was no longer optimal.

When the time came to choose a topic for my master's thesis and my attention was caught by the topic of Kaizen in the office sector at SBB, I wanted to take a closer look at the topic of 'audit'. For me, it was important to investigate how and which tools should be used to find out what potential still exists and with which concrete development steps this can be realised.

There is a lot of information in the literature regarding the implementation of the Kaizen method. However, little useful information can be found about the effectiveness of a Kaizen concept established in an organisation. The measurement of Kaizen quality is completely neglected in the literature. However, my literature research has shown that a Maturity Model is the best way to show whether processes are working well and where further improvements are possible. A Maturity Model can be used to determine the effectiveness and efficiency of processes. To reach the next level in the Maturity Model, concrete improvements have to be made and implemented.

What Fascinates You About the Maturity Model?

The Maturity Model provides valuable information about the continuous development in the different areas of the organisation. Using the Maturity Model, the different units see transparently where they stand in the respective dimensions. The relevant dimensions selected through the literature research (leadership, corporate culture and standards) were reviewed and supplemented with other important dimensions (information and communication as well as order and cleanliness).

The research results have shown that the Maturity Model developed is well suited for gaining versatile information regarding Kaizen development. At the same time, the model shows the development path and promotes the exchange between management, Kaizen supporters and employees. This can promote an increase in acceptance of the new model among managers and employees.

By applying a Maturity Model, benchmarks can be performed and units or organisations can be compared. At the same time, the results obtained can be compared with previous measurements. By introducing a Maturity Model, managers also become more involved in the Kaizen audits. This encourages further development and reflection with and through Kaizen.

What Are Possible Areas of Application?

The Maturity Model developed for the SBB travel centres is geared towards the needs of service companies and is therefore well suited for this use.

As the tests of the Maturity Model showed, the developed tool is mainly aimed at managers and Kaizen agents. Due to their experience and knowledge, they have the necessary skills to facilitate an open and communicative exchange on each selected dimension. It enables leadership to set individual priorities and to continuously improve within the Kaizen system. Since the Maturity Model does not feature clearly defined questions and requires in-depth knowledge from the users, it cannot be applied by every employee.

What Are the Advantages of the Model?

In order to gain the motivation and acceptance of the people involved and to ensure a successful implementation, it is important to show and communicate the added value of the developed tool. Therefore, based on the findings, the added value of the developed model was formulated as follows:

- The Maturity Model developed shows the potential that can be realised with the Kaizen system.
- Managers are positively and intensively involved in the audit process.
- Managers can independently define solutions based on the points from the model and set priorities.
- The regular performance of the audit with the help of the Maturity Model transparently shows the entire Kaizen development of the past years and its results.
- The visual presentation as well as the extension of the development steps was particularly appreciated by the managers. The focus on the defined dimensions was also very positively received.
- The Maturity Model developed is a constructive system that also takes into account the results from previous years.
- In addition, the visual rendering in the form of a spider web offers the possibility for a comparison with a benchmark or with the previous year.

Overall, the Maturity Model was found to be helpful and intelligible, providing a high added value. Based on these results, the implementation of the Maturity Model was recommended for Kaizen agents and supervisors in the SBB travel centres.

Are There Also Weaknesses and Risks That Need to Be Considered When Introducing and Using a Maturity Model?

As the model does not contain defined questions, the degree of subjectivity is high. Moreover, the model is not intended for ordinary employees, but for managers who can interpret results themselves and define resulting improvement measures. This is done on the basis of their experience and appropriate training. Detailed explanations and training on the new tool must be provided to show the objectives and structure of the tool and the audits and thus increase the understanding of the assessment process. To conduct a successful audit, one must be able to ask the right questions. This requires experience and coaching skills.

Where Do You See the Biggest Challenges in the Introduction?
The biggest challenge in introducing a new Kaizen audit tool is to get the stakeholders on board and to motivate them to participate. The focus should be on clearly defined procedures and responsibilities, as well as a transparent audit process and openly communicated goals. In addition, a standardised procedure plays a decisive role. Transparent communication about the reasons for introducing the new tool and pointing out the possibilities for its use will ensure acceptance and motivation among all those involved. This also encourages them to participate. In particular, it is important to create an understanding that the Kaizen audit is not a monitoring of employees, but a tool that identifies opportunities for improvement. The Kaizen audit should be seen as an aid for employees, which additionally supports them in the continuous improvement process.

Thank you Kateryna for the interesting interview about your experience with the development of a Maturity Model for SBB travel centres. Can you give us an overview of the findings of your master's thesis?

My experience in writing my master's thesis showed how important it was that the whole development process of the new Maturity Model in the SBB travel centres was designed in an agile way. This increased the motivation and commitment of the Kaizen agents and all other stakeholders. In doing so, the main principle of Kaizen—employee involvement—could be actively exemplified. After the Maturity Model had been developed and successfully tested, the next step was to develop and implement concrete recommendations for the successful implementation of the new tool.

4.3.1 Importance of the Kaizen Audit and Requirements for the Maturity Model

Within the framework of the research, it was defined that through a Kaizen audit, the changes achieved can be measured and appropriate conclusions can be drawn. With the help of these systematic controls, insights are gained that show whether the measures taken have achieved the desired benefits.

A Kaizen audit is primarily an important tool for managers. A Kaizen audit provides them with information about the status of their division. In the SBB sales sector, for instance, these are the various SBB travel centres. Based on this information, managers can decide for themselves which improvement steps need to be taken. At the same time, a Kaizen audit also motivates or even encourages employees to engage in Kaizen activities. Regarding the research, the following principles of Kaizen audit implementation were formulated:

- It is important to discuss all points in an open conversation.
- The Kaizen supporter acts cooperatively and not dominantly.
- A basis of trust must be built and lived.

The Maturity Model developed for the SBB travel centres is intended to enable the fulfilment of the aforementioned points in order to achieve a maximum positive effect. The requirements mentioned were therefore taken into account when developing the Maturity Model.

An optimally designed Kaizen audit tool should transparently show all audit participants where they are in their development and what they can still improve. In order to reach the next level, continuous improvements must be made. This is the crucial point that is in favour of the introduction of a Maturity Model for the Kaizen audit. By means of the Maturity Model, the different units can see transparently where they stand in the respective dimensions. The literature review has shown the relevant dimensions for Kaizen audits. These are Leadership, corporate culture and standards. These dimensions were reviewed and the following ones were added: information and communication as well as tidiness and cleanliness. The research has shown the following relevant aspects for development in the Kaizen system:

- The development of Kaizen within a travel centre should be set up.
- It makes sense to divide this into several stages.
- Here, visual signposting can be motivating for a team.
- The measurable goals are important for the analysis of the current situation.

By introducing a Maturity Model, managers are also more involved in the Kaizen audits. This will promote future development and reflection with and through Kaizen. Based on the defined requirements for the new Kaizen audit tool, the Maturity Model shown in Fig. 4.22 was developed with six dimensions and five levels.

The short, clear version helps to get a quick overview of the Kaizen development and the related dimensions. The defined levels can be described as follows:

- *Level 1: Few or no Kaizen activities:* Companies and their units do not yet carry out any Kaizen activities.
- *Level 2: Kaizen activities have started:* At this level, the first Kaizen activities are carried out after all employees have been sensitised to the need for change.
- *Level 3: Improvements are made successfully:* With the help of the Kaizen philosophy, process improvements are developed and implemented at this level with the involvement of the employees concerned.
- *Level 4: Improvements are aligned with the goals of the sector:* It is important that improvements are aligned with the goals of the sector. Thus, there are units at this level that align their Kaizen activities with improvement processes that are necessary to achieve the goals.
- *Level 5: Best practices. World class. Kaizen is actively lived:* This corresponds to the highest level of development of a unit within the Kaizen system. Companies that reach this level have the 'best practices' and other companies or units can learn from them.

The insights gained are divided into the different dimensions per level in the model. In order to avoid subjectivity, it is important that the individual characteristics at each level are formulated in a measurable way. The description

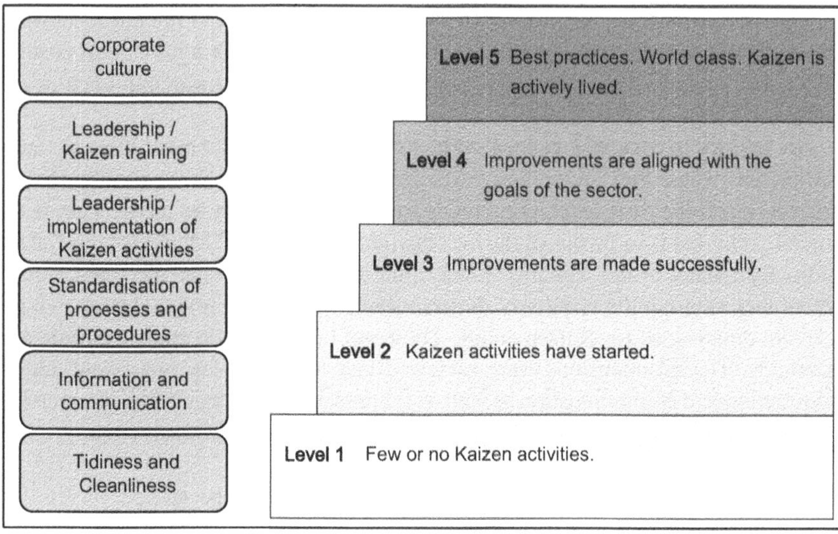

Fig. 4.22 Basic elements of the Kaizen Maturity Model (Source: Kateryna Brönnimann)

of each level also includes recommendations for action, so that the next level can be reached. In a separate Excel file, the stakeholders define their improvement actions for each dimension, which are necessary to reach the next level.

In order to visually display the results of the audit, the results for each dimension are summarised in a Spider Chart. This provides managers and their staff with a quicker overview of the current situation in each dimension. Figure 4.23 shows the graphical representation of the Kaizen audit results as a basis for further discussions.

An important advantage of the Maturity Model is the fact that the results obtained can be easily compared with previous assessments of the same unit or results from other units.

4.3.2 Implementation and Application Possibilities of the Developed Kaizen Maturity Model

The implementation of the Maturity Model for Kaizen agents and supervisors is recommended based on these results. By means of the formulated basic elements (see Fig. 4.24) of the implementation, the understanding of the important aspects of the introduction of the new Kaizen audit tool should be ensured.

As the test of the new Maturity Model showed, the model devised also offers the possibility to carry out self- and external audits in the following format:

- First, a self-audit once a year (max. 1 h).
- Then an external audit once a year (max. 2.5 h).

It makes sense to conduct a short feedback session sometime after an external audit to review and discuss the status and effectiveness of the defined improvement

	actual	last year	comment	measure	deadline	status
Corporate culture	3	2				
Leadership / Kaizen training	3	2				
Leadership / Implementation Kaizen	4	3				
Standardisation of processes	2	3				
Information and communication	2	3				
Tidiness and cleanliness	5	3				

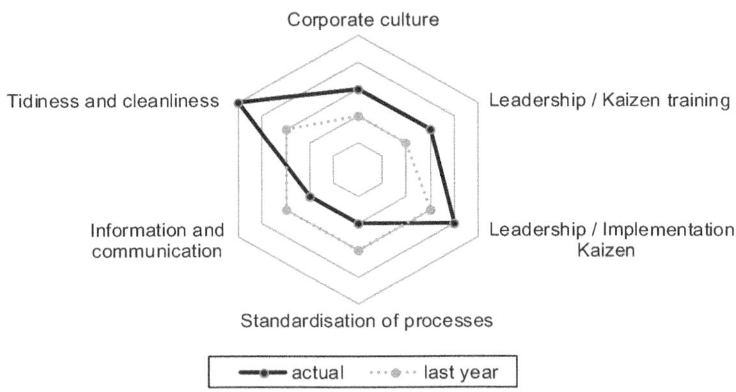

Fig. 4.23 Graphical representation of the Kaizen audit results (Source: Kateryna Brönnimann)

measures (quarterly, max. 20 min). It is important that, regardless of the type of audit, the results are not only communicated transparently to all employees, but can also be reflected upon by them. The developed graphical representation of the results can be used here. It is recommended to place the results on the Kaizen board and then discuss them in a team meeting.

The graphical representation of the results is useful for a comparison with the previous year, for a comparison of self-audit and external audit, for a comparison with other fields or with an external company (benchmark). These comparisons support the search for deviations from the self-assessment. This should be a crucial point for promoting self-reflection, as all employees can transparently see the results in each dimension and with it the comments and improvement measures defined for them at a glance. By means of the presented Kaizen audit results, a successful and effective implementation of the new audit method is supported and promoted due to clear and transparent communication. The results should be communicated personally, e.g., in the form of a meeting. This communication channel also supports understanding and acceptance.

A detailed summary of the findings from Kateryna Brönnimann's master's thesis is published in the book 'Nachhaltige Unternehmensführung, Herausforderungen und Beispiele aus der Praxis' by Kim Oliver Tokarski et al. (2019).

▶ **Recommended Reading** The book 'Six Sigma + Lean Toolset – Mindset zur erfolgreichen Umsetzung von Verbesserungsvorhaben' by Stephan

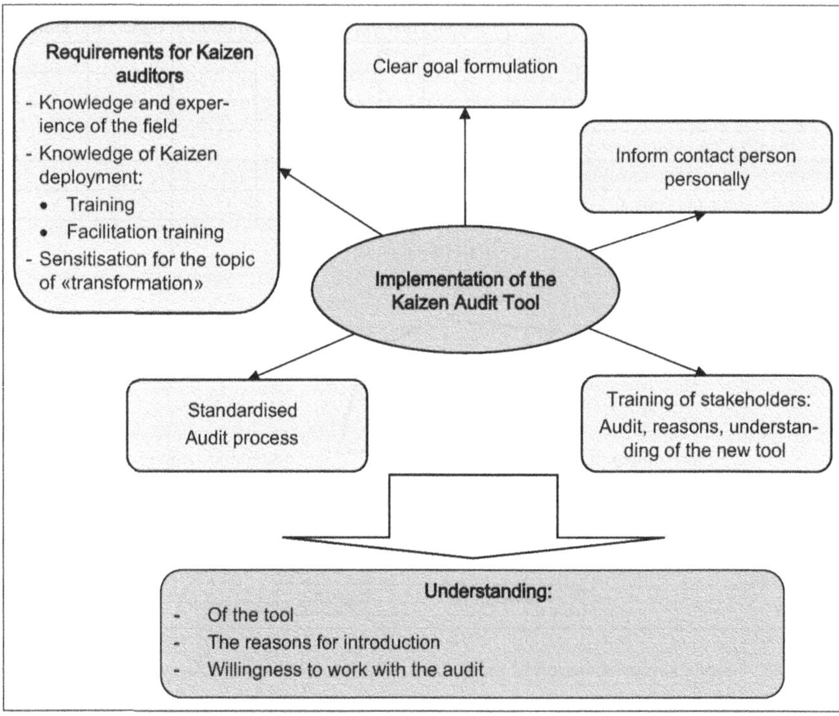

Fig. 4.24 Basic elements of implementing a new Kaizen audit method (Source: Kateryna Brönnimann)

Lunau (2014) offers a comprehensive collection of tools for working on process improvements in the context of Six Sigma projects, and also includes helpful tips for their application in practice.

Recommended Reading A compact overview of the most important Six Sigma tools is also provided in the book 'Six Sigma: Tools, Beispiele, Praxistipps' by Andreas Knecht and Markus Bertschi (2013). It is available in German and is particularly suitable as a reference work for practical application.

References

Knecht, A., & Bertschi, M. (2013). *Six sigma tools – beispiele – praxistipps*. Zürich: Versus.

Lunau, St. (Hrsg) (2014). *Six Sigma + Lean Toolset, Mindset zur erfolgreichen Umsetzung von Verbesserungsprojekten*. Berlin: Springer.

Schmelzer, H., & Sesselmann, W. (2013). *Geschäftsprozessmanagement in der Praxis: Kunden zufrieden stellen, Produktivität steigern, Wert erhöhen*. München: Carl Hanser Verlag.

Tokarski, K., Schellinger, J., & Berchtold, P. (2019). *Nachhaltige Unternehmensführung. Herausforderungen und Beispiele aus der Praxis*. Wiesbaden: Springer Fachmedien.

Influence of Digitalisation on Process Optimisation

5

Digitalisation Is Revolutionising Existing Business Models
Digitalisation enables new, previously unimagined, innovative business models thanks to more direct and faster customer contacts and a larger amount of data. At the same time, however, this development also endangers previously successful companies.

Effects of Digitalisation on Companies
The life cycle of products and services is accelerating and time to market is becoming more paramount. As a result, companies need to become faster and more flexible in developing new business ideas and new products. It is crucial to find the right mix between flexibility and stability in the main activities.

Influence of Digitalisation on Improvement Management
In order to survive in the market with constantly increasing customer demands and ever shorter reaction times, the importance of improvement management continues to grow strongly. There is a particular demand for improvement methods that can be applied quickly and flexibly.

M. Hofmann, *A Holistic Approach to Process Optimisation*, Management for Professionals, https://doi.org/10.1007/978-3-658-34097-1_5

5.1 Digitalisation Is Revolutionising Existing Business Models

In recent years, the topic of digitalisation has rapidly gained in importance and hardly any company can escape this development. The new prospects that arise can be both a great opportunity and a threat to the very existence of a company.

The changes resulting from digitalisation and their effects, such as the rapidly spreading Internet shops, are becoming more and more noticeable. Nevertheless, many people are relatively unaware of the current development and its possible future effects. Overall, the consequences are not yet clearly foreseeable although they will probably be more far-reaching than what can currently be guessed.

5.1.1 What Is Digitalisation?

The origins of digitalisation reach back as far as to the nineteenth century, where it started with the process of digitisation. It began with the conversion of continuous signals into a coding, such as it occurs in the Morse code, for instance. With the binary code and its application in computer technology, the importance of digitisation increased greatly. Digitisation enables the collection of all conceivable data and information. Thanks to rapid technological progress, this data can be collected more and more cost-effectively and in rapidly increasing quantities. This means that companies know their customers better and better and can satisfy their needs and wishes even more precisely. In addition, the new technical possibilities are making customer relationships faster and more direct.

However, the way digitalisation is understood today goes far beyond the technical term of digitisation. According to Hamidian and Krajio (2013), the focus of the digitalisation hype is not the transfer of analogue information to a digital medium, but rather the transfer of people and their living and working worlds to a digital level. People are breaking out of the local offline world and want to be omnipresent, interconnected and 'always-on'. They see themselves as individuals in the ever-present sphere of the digital community. Gassmann and Sutter (2016) write: 'Digitalisation is changing our customer behaviour. It is the driver of the fourth industrial revolution and is changing how people, organisations and industries act and function. Digitalisation is becoming the inner engine of a far-reaching transformation, the extent of which can be predicted technologically, but the social-systematic effects on the economy and society are not nearly grasped'.

The collected data serves to generate added value for the customer and thus also to ensure additional value creation for the company. Data collection follows the following pattern:

- *Generating data:* New technologies are constantly opening up new opportunities to collect data on users, their behaviour and their environment. This can be, for example, information about purchasing behaviour on the Internet or the use of robot vacuum cleaners in the household. This data can either be collected by the company itself or procured via third-party companies.

- *Linking data:* To increase the informative value and usefulness of the collected data from the various sources, they are linked together and put into an editable form.
- *Analyse and visualise data:* In the next processing step, the prepared data is analysed and evaluated. It is crucial that the essential information can be filtered out of the mass of data. Tools that simplify the readability of the data by means of visual representations provide support here.
- *Generate added value from the data:* With the insights gained from the analysis and evaluation of the data, products or services can be further developed and expanded with additional functions. As a result, the wishes and needs of the customers are satisfied even better.

The evaluation and economic use of large amounts of data are to be understood as key components. In this context, the increasing intelligence of algorithms, machines and robots as well as the simpler operation of highly complex technical systems simplify the collection and processing of large amounts of data.

The Stages of Progressive Digitalisation

According to Breyer-Mayländer (2017), the progress of digitalisation can be divided into four stages as shown in Fig. 5.1. These stages differ in the increasing complexity of their interconnectedness.

Due to the increasing interconnection of information systems and the processing of an ever-growing amount of sensitive customer data, the demands on IT security

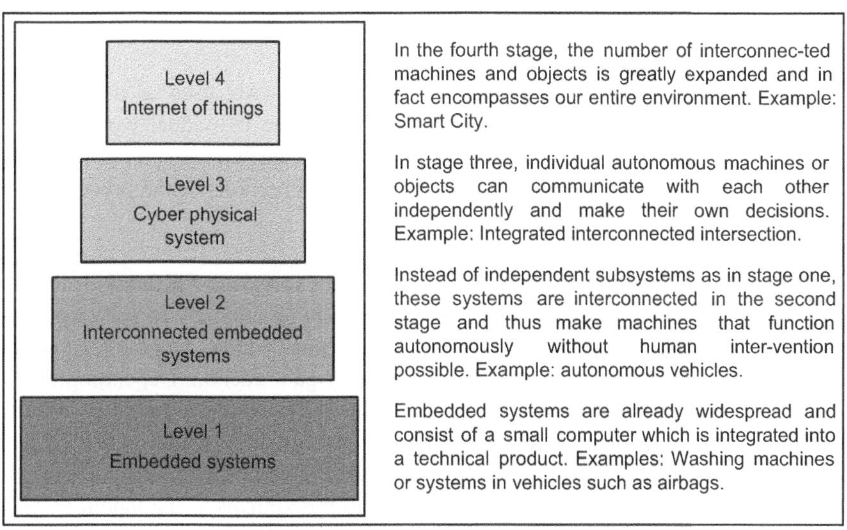

Fig. 5.1 Stages of progressive digitalisation (based on Breyer-Mayländer 2017)

are also rising. This is a decisive prerequisite for the future success and acceptance of digitalisation.

5.1.2 Effects of Digitalisation

Digitalisation is changing our familiar professional and private environment and opening up new, previously unimaginable possibilities. This is a continuous change based on ever faster and more powerful data and communication systems. Certain changes, such as controlling the heating via mobile phone, have already become an integral part of our everyday lives in recent years. But this is only the beginning. With the rapidly progressing development, further changes with profound effects will follow.

Effects on the Labour Market

All these changes have a direct or at least indirect impact on the labour market and our daily work. Even today, almost everyone uses digital devices at work. For example, work instructions and checklists can be retrieved quickly everywhere thanks to progressive interconnectivity, and work reports are increasingly being recorded directly electronically. Many tasks performed by humans today will be taken over by intelligent machines in the future.

With regard to the expected future effects on the labour market, Gassmann and Sutter (2016) focus on the following two scenarios:

- *The tool scenario:* In this scenario, technology is mainly used in a supporting role. The necessary decisions are still made by skilled workers who monitor and control the machines. This requires a high level of expertise and experience among the employees involved.
- *The automation scenario:* Here, technology is not only used as a support. It actively takes the lead and takes over control of the individual work steps. It makes decisions independently based on complex algorithms. In this scenario, the human is guided by the machine through clear instructions or the processes run completely without humans.

It can be assumed that neither one of these two scenarios will prevail. Rather, mixed forms will emerge depending on the type and complexity of the respective situation and task. With the increasing technical possibilities, however, it can be assumed that the automation scenario will strongly gain traction. Depending on the scenario, the effects on the labour market will differ. Either way, they will be enormous, and certain activities performed by humans will be eliminated. If jobs are lost due to this change, this is referred to as technological unemployment.

However, technological change does not only pose threats to the labour market, but also creates a variety of opportunities and new possibilities. For example, many new jobs are being created in the IT sector to master the new technologies. It will be crucial that the training and know-how of the workforce meet the new challenges of the working world and the labour market.

Trends in Digitalisation

The effects of digitalisation that can be perceived today are only the tip of the iceberg. Further profound changes and their social consequences can only be vaguely estimated today, if at all. The most important trends with the potential for profound changes include, for example:

- *Blockchain technology:* This technology enables fast and secure transactions between computers and at the same time offers increased protection against data manipulation. Among other things, blockchain technology became known through cryptocurrencies such as Bitcoin. In the future, thanks to blockchain technology, intermediaries such as banks may become superfluous for payment transactions.
- *Cloud computing:* Instead of installing IT infrastructures on local computers and storing data and programmes locally, these are provided, executed and stored in the so-called cloud. The required systems and data are accessed via the Internet. Thanks to cloud computing, location-independent access to required data is made possible. Further advantages of the cloud are the demand-oriented, dynamic adjustment of computing power and billing based on the resources actually used (computing power, storage space and data transfer). In addition, the efficiency of overlapping activities between different companies can be increased by jointly accessing data and algorithms from the cloud.
- *Big Data:* This is the technology for analysing very large, often unstructured amounts of data. Big data can be used, for example, to analyse the buying behaviour of customers. This makes it possible to give purchase recommendations that are individually tailored to the customer. Big data also helps to identify trends in society. Newspaper articles and social media are analysed for this purpose, for instance. Another example is interconnected devices. These sometimes generate large amounts of diagnostic data. Using Big Data, the device manufacturer can analyse how the devices are used and how to improve customer benefits in the next generation of devices. It is also possible to predict when a device should be serviced.
- *Cognitive computing:* In cognitive computing, the computer takes over tasks that previously had to be performed by humans. Examples include service hotlines, autonomous driving, automated stock trading, credit card fraud detection, facial recognition and expert systems in the medical field. The basis for cognitive computing is artificial intelligence, machine learning, human language recognition and machine vision. Cognitive computing opens up the following new possibilities, among others:
  - Completion of routine tasks by the computer, which were previously carried out by human service staff.
  - Analysis and processing of written and spoken texts by computer.
  - Analysis and processing of video and image material by computer.

  - Processing of practically unlimited amounts of text, video and image data in a short time. Example: Automated search of film archives for key scenes.
  - Making expert knowledge available mechanically. Unlike rare human experts, the machine expert can be copied as often as desired and thus offers unlimited availability.
- *3D printing:* Also called additive manufacturing. This is the computer-controlled, layer-by-layer creation of a three-dimensional body. With 3D printers available today, it is possible to print bodies made of plastics, ceramics or metals. 3D printing makes it possible to produce prototypes relatively quickly and inexpensively. Furthermore, the use of 3D printing for small batches or one-off production can be economically superior to traditional manufacturing processes. 3D printing can also eliminate the need to stock spare parts that are rarely in demand. Another advantage of 3D printing is that transports are reduced because products can be printed directly on the customer's premises.

5.1.3 Effects of Digitalisation on Business Models

The more direct and faster contacts to customers as well as the large amount of available electronic data are changing the markets worldwide and across all sectors. This can be seen, for example, in the countless Internet shops that are springing up at an explosive rate. In addition, companies from the so-called new technology such as Uber or Airbnb are changing established industries with new innovative business models.

This inevitably leads to traditional business models and corporate structures having to be adapted or, in the worst case, becoming completely superfluous. Due to the simple and direct customer contact via the Internet, we can already observe that many business models that are based on the mediation between manufacturers and customers will become partly redundant or replaced by machines. These include, for example, the mediation of air travel in travel agencies or the provision of information by telephone.

Digital Transformation

Existing companies must deal intensively with the changes in order to not be surprised and overtaken by the development. According to Gassmann and Sutter (2016) the following fourteen points are crucial for mastering the digital transformation:

1. *Customer knowledge at the core:* Customers and their needs must be at the centre of a company's activities. By means of feedback loops, these needs can be efficiently grasped. The better they are satisfied, the greater the market success and the added value of the company.
2. *Developing a strong vision:* A strong vision helps to bundle the existing forces and enables the unified alignment of the existing resources.

3. *Developing digital business models:* The existing business models must be reviewed and adapted to the changed framework conditions.
4. *Promoting high-performance teams:* Self-directing and interdisciplinary teams can deal with complex issues in a more targeted and efficient manner.
5. *Pushing for permanent learning:* Verify assumptions by building and testing prototypes. It is important that mistakes are allowed to be made. This promotes learning and quickly provides new insights.
6. *Strengthening agility in development:* Development in so-called sprints (see Sect. 3.1.5 on agile management) and the interactive procedure with close customer contact are increasingly replacing the sequential waterfall model, which consists of the phases: Requirements analysis, design and implementation.
7. *Overcoming silos:* In order to be able to implement digitalisation initiatives, it is necessary to collaborate across existing company boundaries.
8. *Energising the whole organisation:* A committed development team alone is not enough. The entire organisation must be won over to the new alignment in order to pursue the goals together and to avoid internal trench warfare.
9. *Putting up tents instead of palaces:* It is better to put up tents quickly and take them down again if unsuccessful than to plan a perfect palace that will last for eternity. Agility, learning and flexibility replace planning.
10. *Promoting a lean start-up mentality:* Instead of developing big long-term plans, a stronger orientation towards actions is required. The design, build and test cycles must be completed quickly. In addition, customer feedback must be obtained on a continuous basis.
11. *Building strategic partnerships:* If new things are to be created, cooperation is more important than opposition in the world of networks.
12. *Winning the battle for talent:* Highly qualified IT developers and programmers in particular are highly competitive on the labour market. Without these specialists, however, new projects in the field of digitalisation cannot be implemented.
13. *Realising quick wins:* Especially in long-term transformations, it is necessary to realise and communicate short-term progress as well.
14. *Communication, communication:* It is crucial that the reasons, goals and progress of the digital transformation are highlighted at every opportunity.

Adaptation of the Business Model

The right business model is important for the success of a company. According to Gassmann and Sutter (2016) a successful business model addresses the issues of value proposition, revenue mechanism and value-added chain. These main points remain unchanged even in the age of digitalisation. However, it is crucial that existing business models, driven by the new technological possibilities, are continuously reconsidered and adapted to the new circumstances. The three main points of the business model and the influence of digitalisation can be described as follows:

Value Proposition—What Is Offered to the Customer?
The focus of every business model is the customer and their needs. The better the customer's needs can be met, the more successful a product or service will be on the market. With the new technical possibilities, completely new opportunities arise through more direct customer contact.

Revenue Mechanism—How Is Value Achieved?
How can profit be generated with the business model? This question is not always easy to answer, especially in the case of new business models created by digitalisation. As a result, innovative ideas often remain unsuccessful despite great customer benefits.

Value-Added Chain—How Is the Service Produced?
This item concerns the question of how the product or service is created and made available to the customer. Due to the increasing direct customer contact via the Internet, the rising demands on availability and the customers' need for ever faster delivery, this item is becoming more and more important.

5.2 Effects of Digitalisation on Companies

Unchanged from the situation prior to digitalisation, the business processes will also have to be defined and continuously developed in the future based on the value-added chain defined in the business model. However, the requirements for error-free and rapid processing of customer orders and all associated activities will continue to increase. Fast and error-free processing of customer orders can only be ensured through clearly defined and functioning workflows. In addition, the consequences of errors in the digital environment are often more serious than before digitisation due to the more closely timed processes. Nowadays, for example, customers are hardly willing to wait longer for the ordered goods due to a failure in the procurement of an online shop. Instead, they switch to another shop.

Furthermore, the intensive handling of sensitive customer data requires clear internal guidelines to ensure compliance with the legal standards and to protect customer data. A data leak can seriously damage a company's reputation and, in extreme cases, even threaten its very existence.

The digital transformation with its partly unclear effects demands more flexible organisational structures from companies with greater freedom to act for employees and short decision-making paths. At first glance, these requirements clash with the demand for clearly structured and error-free processes, which require a certain stability of the environment. The challenge in the future will be to find the right balance between flexibility and stability for the individual activities in the company.

Figure 5.2 shows that a more flexible approach is particularly advantageous in the development of new business models and their implementation up to market launch. It makes the development process more efficient and shortens the time until the new products or services are introduced to the market. The technical term for the time

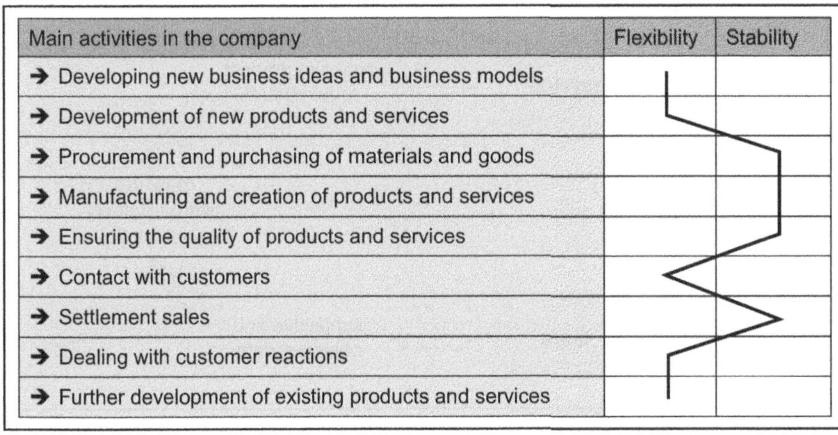

Fig. 5.2 Flexibility versus stability of the main activities in the company

until market launch is called 'time to market'. A high degree of flexibility is also advantageous when dealing with customers and in the continuous development of products and services. In contrast, the advantages of stable processes outweigh the disadvantages in the creation and sale of products and services. They ensure the correctness of the processes and the quality of the products.

The Development of New Products and Services

This increasing flexibility is particularly evident in the development of new products and services. Agile methods such as Scrum are increasingly being used in this area. These methods enable faster implementation, a reduction in time to market, an increase in quality and a more targeted use of available resources. Instead of complex projects, the rapid development of prototypes is increasingly preferred. These can be further improved within a short time thanks to direct customer feedback, as shown in Fig. 5.3. This necessary customer feedback can be obtained at test markets, for instance. In software development, these short efficient development cycles lead to release cycles becoming shorter and shorter. In extreme cases, even several releases per day are possible. Example: Facebook Front End is released three times a day. The mobile app is released every fortnight.

5.2.1 Impact on Organisations

The changes driven by the progressive digitalisation have a strong impact on the organisation of companies. In particular, the changed behaviour of customers and the processing and evaluation of the mass of available data require a lean, flexible organisation and an adaptable management system. Such an organisation is characterised by the following features:

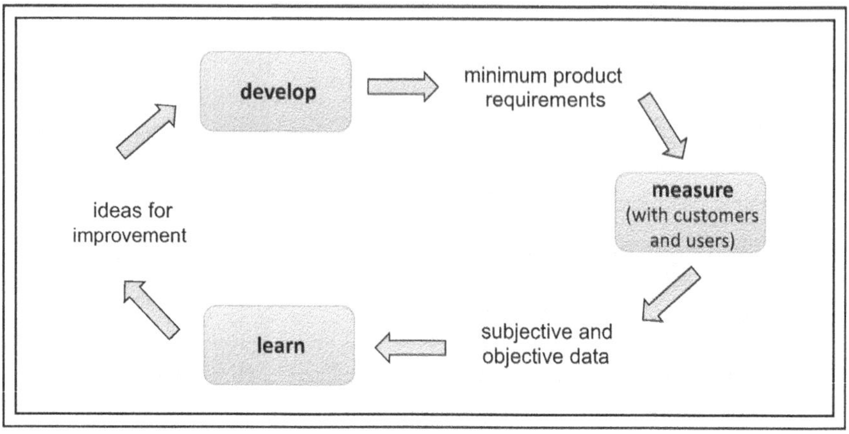

Fig. 5.3 Development cycle (based on Rins after Anderson 2015)

- *Flat organisation:* The absence of hierarchical levels promotes the more direct involvement of all participants and encourages their own initiative. This allows changes to be tackled and implemented more quickly.
- *Cross-functional teams:* Responsibility for managing independent work areas is increasingly being transferred to cross-functional teams. This includes, among other things, making pending decisions and implementing them within the framework of the company-wide goals.
- *Orientation towards the customer:* The organisation is focused on creating added value for customers and satisfying their needs as precisely as possible.
- *Short decision-making and communication channels:* Decision-making authority is delegated to the responsible divisions and teams. This allows for quick and flexible actions. At the same time, thanks to the inclusion of new means of communication, the available information is distributed quickly.

These characteristics are best fulfilled with an agile management approach (see Sect. 3.1.5 agile methods). The agile approach offers the necessary flexibility in corporate management and in the new and further development of business models, products and services. Agile management is becoming increasingly important today and is now prevalent far beyond the IT sector.

5.2.2 Effects on the Work Processes

However, the increasing spread of agile management does not mean that standardised work processes with detailed work instructions and clear checklists will no longer be needed in the future. On the contrary: In order to be able to make the new products and services available to the customer in the desired high quality and in the shortest possible time, effective and efficient work processes are needed that can be quickly adapted to changing requirements. In this area, improvement methods such as Kaizen or Six Sigma continue to gain in importance, but these methods also need to become more flexible and efficient in order to be able to react to rapidly changing customer needs within a reasonable period of time.

In order for this flexibilisation of work processes to function in everyday life, not only the continuous improvement of processes is needed, but also new knowledge-management systems that meet the increased requirements in work processes. Processes are increasingly supported by new technologies, making them more sophisticated, interconnected and complex. Fully integrated systems contain the process steps from development to sales and can be accessed by employees and in some cases even by customers at any time. At the same time, with digitalisation, simple work processes are increasingly automated and carried out by machines. As a result, interaction between humans and machines is becoming increasingly important. In addition, IT skills are needed more and more to control and optimise work processes.

5.3 Influence of Digitalisation on Improvement Management

Agile approaches will become much more important in the future. However, this does not mean that process and improvement management will lose importance in turn. Agility supports the creation of something new, and clear work processes help to implement this 'new' in ongoing operations with the required quality.

The new technologies lead to a strong acceleration, both in the creation of products and services within the company and in the exchange with customers. Whereas it used to take one to two weeks to order and deliver photo prints, this can now be done in one to two days thanks to the Internet. For companies, this means that their business processes have to be even more effective and efficient. In addition, problems and errors in work processes have even greater consequences. For example, problems in the system immediately have a negative impact on delivery times, and poor IT security in dealing with customer data quickly leads to negative headlines.

These increasing requirements lead to improvement management becoming even more important in the future. In order to ensure functioning work processes in the company at all times, the time factor is also becoming an increasingly strong driver in improvement management. In detail, this means:

1. Early detection of problems:
   - Anchoring of a measurement system with early-warning indicators.
   - Active feedback from the employees involved.
2. Addressing the identified problems quickly:
   - Set up efficient structures for guiding and controlling improvement management.
   - Collect improvement topics in a topic repository.
   - Prioritise issues with a high benefit.

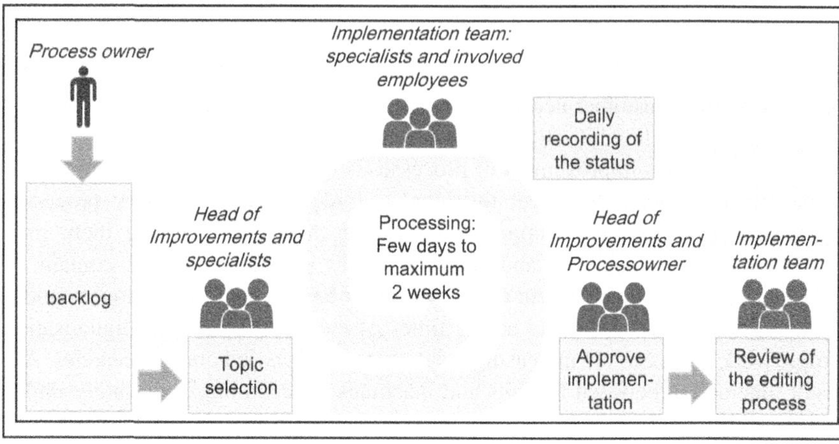

Fig. 5.4 Improvement management in the age of digitalisation

3. Processing and implementation in cross-functional implementation teams:
   - Implementation in combined teams of specialists for process optimisation and employees involved in the process.
   - Short, intensive processing time; optimisations are to be realised directly in the processing phase.
4. Approval and measurement of the results:
   - Approval of the results directly after processing by those responsible for the process.
   - Improvements are communicated and implemented directly after approval.
   - Measuring the cost and benefit of the improvement.

Which improvement method is used is not as significant. What is essential is that the method is adapted to today's environment. This means that processing and implementation must be faster and more agile. Figure 5.4 shows the processing of improvement projects in the age of digitalisation.

This process for handling improvement projects borrows heavily from the agile approach to handling projects. The essential elements of the process are:

- *Backlog:* The backlog is used to collect the improvement topics that are recorded on an ongoing basis. For each topic, a fact sheet and an assessment of the cost and benefits are to be prepared. Only projects with a positive cost-benefit ratio are included in the topic repository.
- *Topic selection:* The choice of topics is made on an ongoing basis by the person overall responsible for improvement management together with the specialists.
- *Processing the topics:* The topics are worked on jointly by the technical specialists and the employees involved in the workflow. The technical specialists contribute their methodological and IT expertise.

- *Daily recording of the status:* While working on a project, the team discusses the status of the work progress daily and decides on the further procedure. In case of problems, the head of the improvement project is consulted for support.
- *Approve implementation:* Approval is carried out by the head of improvement management and the process owner of the processed workflow.
- *Review of the editing process:* After completion of the processing of each improvement project, the implementation team discusses the procedure and records optimisations for the processing of future projects.

5.3.1 The Roles Involved

To ensure that improvement projects are processed quickly and efficiently, the following roles are involved:

- *Company management:* Responsible for anchoring improvement management in the company and ensuring the necessary framework conditions for implementation.
- *Process owners:* Responsible for the smooth running of their processes. They monitor the processes and register new improvement projects if necessary. They are responsible for implementing the improvements.
- *Improvement Manager:* Reports directly to the company management and is responsible for the processing of open improvement projects. Together with the specialists, they prioritise the projects to be worked on and support the implementation team in their processing.
- *Specialists:* Have methodological expertise in the various methods and procedures. With increasing digitalisation, specialists from the IT sector are becoming more and more important for support.
- *Employees involved:* Are involved in the process and, together with the specialists, form the implementation team.

5.3.2 Measurement of the Optimisations Achieved

The optimisations achieved are measured directly when the respective improvement projects are approved by the process owner and the improvement manager. As shown in Fig. 5.5 the cost and the benefit of the individual projects are continuously added up in a graphical representation. This makes it possible to see the effect of the implemented improvements at any time.

In addition, an assessment of the processes with the Maturity Model should be carried out once a year. This allows an assessment of the state of the processes and the progress made since the last survey. For a description of the Maturity Model, see Sect. 4.2).

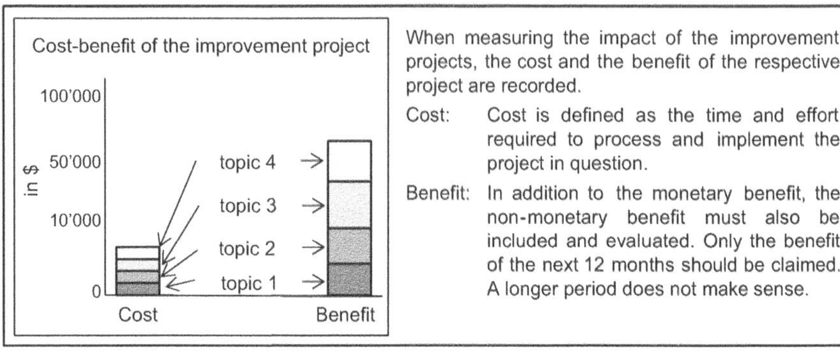

Fig. 5.5 Measuring the effect of the improvement

> **Recommended Reading** In the book 'Digitale Transformation im Unternehmen gestalten' Oliver Gassmann and Phillipp Sutter (2016) describe the impact of digitalisation on companies. They show how companies can react to these changes and which measures are necessary to master the challenges.

References

Anderson, B. (2015). *Plan to learn faster*, June 12. 2015. Retrieved 17 of December 2020 from http://radar.oreilly.com/2015/06/plan-to-learn-faster.html

Breyer-Mayländer, T. (2017). *Management 4.0: Den digitalen Wandel erfolgreich meistern: Das Kursbuch für Führungskräfte*. München: Carl Hanser Verlag.

Gassmann, O., & Sutter, P. (2016). *Digitale Transformation im Unternehmen gestalten: Geschäftsmodelle, Erfolgsfaktoren, Handlungsanweisungen, Fallstudien*. München: Carl Hanser Verlag.

Hamidian, K., & Krajio, C. (2013). Die Digitalisierung: Status quo. In F. Keuper et al. (Eds.), *Digitalisierung und innovation: Planung, Entstehung, Entwicklungsperspektiven*. Springer-Fachmedien: Wiesbaden.

Part II

Practice

6 Putting Process Optimisation in Practice

Practical Examples for Successful Implementation
The concrete implementation of process optimisation is illustrated on the basis of successful improvement projects from practice. The improvement methods described in Chap. 3 and the tools presented in Chap. 4 are applied systematically.

Practical Experience of an Expert on the Kaizen Method
Stephan Spada is a project manager for Kaizen in the Infrastructure division at the Swiss Federal Railways (SBB). He is jointly responsible for the introduction of Kaizen Office (Administration) and has been leading large Kaizen process optimisation workshops for years. Stephan Spada reports on his experiences from his everyday professional life and shows the concrete implementation based on a current improvement project.

M. Hofmann, *A Holistic Approach to Process Optimisation*, Management for Professionals, https://doi.org/10.1007/978-3-658-34097-1_6

6.1 Practical Examples for Successful Implementation

This chapter deals with the implementation of improvement projects in practice. Based on concrete projects, the structured process is shown step by step. The improvement methods described in Chap. 3 and the tools presented in Chap. 4 are applied systematically. Notes on stumbling blocks and practical tips complement the detailed explanations.

The selected examples come from various realised improvement projects of the last few years. For a clear presentation, the examples have been somewhat simplified and put into a uniform format.

6.1.1 Example 1: Financial Planning for Multiple Locations

Huber Ltd. is an industrial company with several locations in Switzerland. For future corporate management, a proactive financial plan is prepared annually for the next 5 years.

In the production division of Huber Ltd., which includes various decentralised locations and interdependencies, planning is particularly complex. The 'Head of Finance Production' is responsible for planning in this sector. His team is represented by one employee on each site. These employees are responsible for ensuring that the financial tasks of the respective site are carried out. Figure 6.1 shows the organisation of the finances of the production division of Huber Ltd.

Initial Situation

The framework for multi-year planning is provided by the overarching planning guidelines set by the company's head office. These include, among other things, company-wide parameters such as future inflation rates, exchange rates or target margins. In addition, the overarching deadlines as well as a uniform tool for recording the results of the planning of the individual divisions are specified. Based on the central specifications, planning in the production division is carried out in the following steps:

1. The employee of the head office prepares a schedule coordinated with the division management as well as a detailed entry form in Microsoft Excel. The form includes all account types and cost centres of the production division. They send the schedule and the form to the employees at the various locations.
2. The employees at the sites work out the necessary data together with the local site managers and complete the Excel file. If necessary, they independently expand the file with rows or columns to add new accounts and cost centres.
3. The completed Excel files are returned by the employees of the sites to the employee of the head office at the specified time.

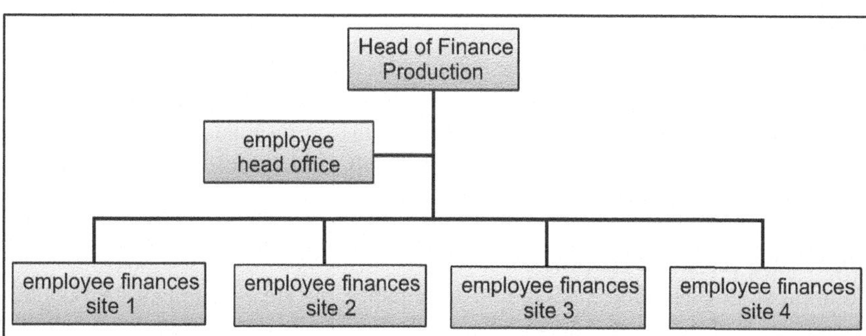

Fig. 6.1 Finance organisation of the production division of Huber Ltd.

4. The employee of the head office compiles the files of the individual sites. In doing so, they check the completeness of the entries and whether the goals set by the management have been met. Errors and discrepancies are reported back to the respective employees so that the necessary corrections can be made.
5. They then allocate the planned costs of the central division's central functions to the individual products and sites and convey them to the employees at the sites.
6. The employees at the sites complete the allocated costs of the central divisions in the form and send it back.
7. The employee of the head office again creates an overall view, which they discuss with the Head of Finance Production. The Head of Finance Production decides on any necessary adjustments. These are entered directly into the file.
8. The result of the planning is presented for discussion and approval by the Head of Finance Production in the management meeting of the production division.
9. The planning of the production division approved by the division management is forwarded to the company headquarters.

The many adjustments that occur with this procedure result in a lot of work, especially for the employee of the head office. In addition, the manual changes in the data entry forms often cause errors. This leads to incorrect results in the stored formulas, for example, in the calculation of social security contributions. Correcting these errors in turn causes a lot of additional work and delays. Discrepancies often arise during consolidation because the individual sites recorded the deliveries differently due to a lack of coordination between the employees involved. As a result of these problems, the deadlines for submission to the management of the production division and to the company headquarters cannot be met.

Based on the team-internal recording of the workload, which has been carried out for a year, the time required for the planning of last year can be determined. The total effort amounts to 51 days and is divided among the team as follows:

- 3 days Head of Finance Production
- 18 days employee of the head office
- Between 7 and 8 days per employee at the site (total of 30 days for all four employees)

Furthermore, the deadline for the submission to the company headquarters could not be met last year. The submission only took place on 29 September instead of 22 September, as was previously specified. This corresponds to a delay of five working days. When measured from the kick-off, which took place on 7 August, this results in a total lead time of 35 days.

Procedure for the Solution

To improve this situation quickly and sustainably, the Head of Finance Production organises a half-day workshop with his staff. The content of the workshop is divided into the following five steps:

1. Determine the starting point and the question.
2. Determine fields of action.
3. Work on fields of action.
4. Implement improvements.
5. Check effect.

1. Determine the starting point and the question

At the beginning of the workshop, the Head of Finance Production defines the starting point and the questions together with his team. The results are recorded on the flipchart shown in Fig. 6.2, which is hung on the wall so that all the points are clearly visible. In addition, it is noted which topics are not the focus of the workshop. This initial discussion serves to strengthen the common understanding of the question and to define the goals. It lays the foundation for a goal-oriented and successful approach. The clearly visible poster on the wall serves as a guide during the entire workshop and prevents the participants from drifting away from the set goals.

2. Determine fields of action

After defining the issue, the next step is to identify the causes of the existing difficulties. For this purpose, the Head of Finance Production uses the Ishikawa Diagram as a tool. This tool is described in detail in Sect. 4.1.7. After the prepared blank diagram is hung on the wall, they start to identify the causes of the existing problems together with their staff. These are categorised according to the six overarching themes. The prepared Ishikawa Diagram can be seen in Fig. 6.3.

The jointly created Ishikawa Diagram shows that the majority of the difficulties occur in two areas. Some of the causes are attributed to the 'human' area (know-how

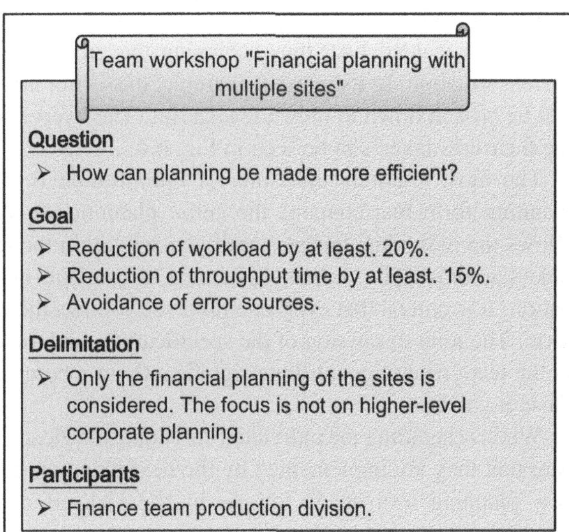

Fig. 6.2 Starting position for optimising planning with multiple site

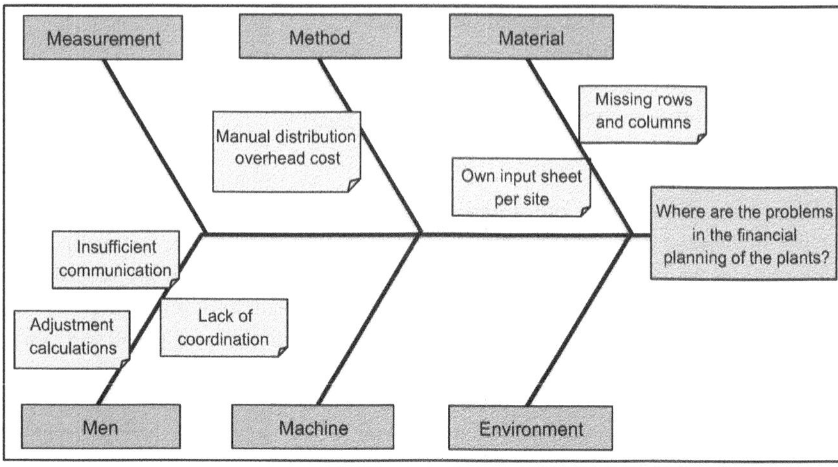

Fig. 6.3 Ishikawa Diagram for optimising planning with multiple sites

and communication) and others to the material area (various sheets and lack of databases).

3. Work on fields of action

In the next step, the causes found are recorded in a table as fields of action and described in more detail. The list serves as a basis for the joint development of concrete proposals for solutions. These are also entered in the table. It is important for the processing and implementation of the individual fields of action that a responsible person and a deadline for the implementation of the solution are determined. If there are many and complex fields of action, it is advisable to prioritise them according to importance. This ensures that the fields of action with the greatest impact are tackled first, thus achieving the greatest possible improvement of the current situation. In the present example, this is not necessary because the problems can be broken down to only a few causes. The overview of the fields of action with the measures taken can be seen in Fig. 6.4.

The most important measure for optimisation is the creation of an integrated planning form that contains the entire planning of the production division. This allows the individual business transactions within the division to be calculated and linked automatically. It reduces manual adjustments and saves time during consolidation. It is crucial that everyone involved follows the rules when working with the form. The joint discussion of the specifications and the release of the planning form in the team meeting contribute significantly to a common understanding among all those involved.

When scheduling the individual solutions, the Head of Finance Production makes sure that they are implemented by the next planning phase. The goal is to have the new planning form ready for use by the kick-off of the multi-year planning on

Field of action	Description	Solution approach	Responsible	Deadline	Done
Various Tools	A separate form exists for each site. This makes consolidation difficult and time-consuming.	Creation of an integrated form with separate work-sheets for the sites and the head office.	employee of the head office	5.8.	✗
Adjustment calculations	The employees at the sites adjust formulas and cells in the form without consultation.	No formulas may be adjusted. Adjustments are only made by the employee of the head office.	All employees	ongoing	✗
Lack of coordination	In the case of mutual deliveries between the different sites, no reconciliation takes place.	All deliveries are entered in a central input sheet by the respective delivering party.	employees finances sites	5.8.	✗
Manual allocation overhead costs	The manual allocation of overhead costs is error-prone and costly.	Include automatic allocation in the new integrated form.	employee of the head office	5.8.	✗
Missing rows and columns	New input fields are partly missing in the entry forms and are added manually during entry.	Entry form is released in the team meeting. It is checked whether all input fields are available.	Head of Finance Production	8.8.	✗

Fig. 6.4 Fields of action for optimising planning with multiple sites

5 August. The discussion and release of the form is scheduled for the team meeting on 8 August.

4. Implement improvements

To ensure implementation, all deadlines specified in the workshop are included in the team's task list. This allows progress to be reviewed and discussed on a regular basis.

The greatest effort in the implementation of the improvement measures decided upon is caused by the creation of the new integrated planning form. However, this measure also promises to provide the greatest benefits. Only with the integrated form is a structured and standardised approach to planning possible.

5. Check effect

To check the effectiveness of the measures adopted, the Head of Finance Production takes stock with their team after the completion of the long-term planning. Overall, the feedback is very positive. All those involved have the impression of having experienced less stress. In addition, they are of the opinion that they have produced a more reliable plan and have done so with significantly less coordination effort than a year earlier.

The commitment of the employees at the sites can also be regarded as positive. No one changed or overwrote an existing formula in the planning form or added more rows and columns. The idea expressed in the workshop that all formulas in the form should be protected against change proved to be unnecessary. This experience shows that solutions that are developed in the team are supported and accepted by the whole team. As a result, excessive regulation and monitoring can often be dispensed with.

The evaluation of the time expenditure supports the positive impression. Instead of a processing time of 51 working days, the team spent only 39 days this year on the complete preparation of the planning. This corresponds to a reduction of 12 days or about 24% compared to the previous year. The employee of the head office benefitted the most from the improvements. For the sake of completeness, it should be mentioned here that the employee of the head office spent about seven additional days to prepare the new planning form. However, this is a one-time expense that has already paid off in the first year and will no longer be incurred next year.

It is gratifying that the deadline for the submission to the company headquarters was met without any problems. Already 2 days before the official submission, the planning could be released to the management of the production division. This corresponds to a reduction of the lead time by seven working days (−20%) compared to the previous year.

Practical Tips

1. For the duration of the workshop, appoint a person responsible for ensuring the focus of the team. Among other things, this person monitors time management and the focus on the improvement topic. I generally rotate this role within the team so that each staff member can gain experience.
2. It is important that the team leader in the team workshop does not take any special position in the processing of the improvement. Only if all participants are equally involved will the workshop lead to the desired result.
3. Work with paper and pens and pin the results to the wall. Even though it is tempting to record the results directly in the computer, this should be refrained from. Working with paper and pens facilitates the involvement of all participants and supports creativity in finding solutions.

6.1.2 Example 2: Optimising the Preparation of Documents for the Project Committee

A supplier to the automotive industry has recently decided to build an additional production hall at the existing site in Italy. This production hall is scheduled to start operations in 2 years. The cost estimate for the new building is around 20 million euros. The construction work was assigned to a general contractor. To implement the project, a project organisation was set up under the leadership of the site manager.

To monitor and manage this project, a monthly project committee meeting is held at the site in Italy. The following persons take part: the site manager, the production manager, the project manager, the responsible financial manager of the group, the representative of the group and the construction supervisor. Before the meeting, the required documents are prepared, printed and sent out. This is done at least 1 week before the meeting so that there is enough time to send the documents by post to all participants not working at the site. These are the representative of the group, the responsible financial manager of the group and the construction supervisor.

Initial Situation

After the first meetings, it becomes apparent that the effort required to prepare the numerous documents takes up a lot of time and that the coordination between the participants is not optimal. In addition, there are often last-minute additions or changes that have to be incorporated into the documents at short notice. Based on the feedback received, the site manager has decided to carry out an improvement project on the topic of 'Optimising the preparation of documents for the project committee'.

The basis for the improvement project is recorded by the site manager with a fact sheet. This is shown in Fig. 6.5.

Procedure of the Workshop

During the workshop, the site manager takes the role of the facilitator. First, they present the initial situation and the goals on the basis of the previously prepared fact sheet and discuss these with the persons participating in the workshop. Then they post the planned workshop schedule on the wall in a clearly visible position as shown in Fig. 6.6.

The process they have chosen follows the normal procedure for processing and implementing simple improvement projects and does not contain any significant special features. It is crucial that the individual steps are adhered to consistently and that no hasty conclusions are drawn. Otherwise, there is a risk of overlooking important causes and connections.

1. Actual-condition analysis

As a basis for recording the current situation, the site manager places on the table all the documents sent out from the last project committee meeting. The documents cover five different topics. These were prepared by three different people. The site

Topic of the workshop:
Optimisation of the preparation of documents for the project committee

Initial situation /problem description

- The documents for the meeting do not meet the requirements and the coordination during the preparation is poor.
- The preparation of the documents takes too long and there are often subsequent adjustments.

Participants

- Site manager
- Production manager
- Project manager
- Representative of the group
- Financial manager of the group
- Construction supervisor

Delimitation

- In Scope: coordination with partners from the group and the external construction company.
- Out of Scope: preparation of documents for regular meetings (e.g., weekly production meeting).

Realisation

Location:	Factory in Italy
Date / time:	17.3.: 08:00 –12:00
Final presentation:	17.3.: 11:30 –12:00

Effect / Goal

- Reduction of the time required to create the documents by 30%.
- Prevention of re-dispatch.
- Better coordination of the documents and therefore better quality of the contents.

Signature sponsor:

Site Manager F. Meyer

Fig. 6.5 Fact sheet 'Optimisation of the preparation of documents for the project committee'

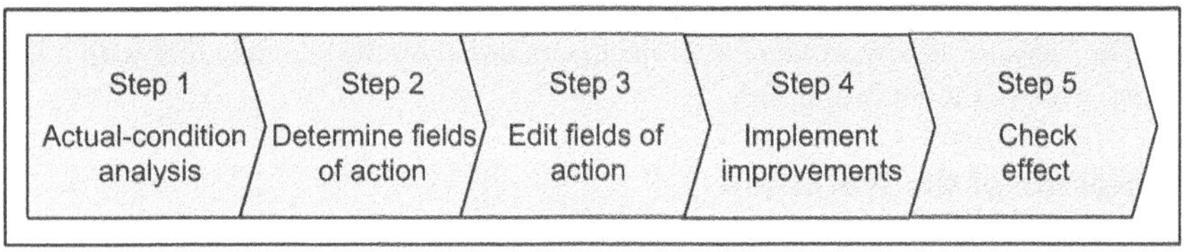

Fig. 6.6 Process of the workshop 'Optimisation of the preparation of documents for the project committee'

manager then draws a table on the board to record the most important facts together. The fully completed table can be seen in Fig. 6.7.

The current situation shows that the preparation of the various documents takes a lot of time and that various changes and additions have to be made shortly before the meeting. In addition, the feedback from the participants shows that the contents of the individual topics are not optimally coordinated. The insights into the current situation gained in the workshop are summarised here:

1. The total time needed to prepare the documents is 16 h. Out of these, 6 h alone are used for last-minute adjustments and updates.

Topic	Respon-sible	Time of preparation	Content	Time required
A Overview status project	Project manager	- 10 days before meeting - Update for meeting	- Overall project view - Schedule - Critical issues	2 hours + 1 hour for Update
B Detail topics project	Project manager	- 10 days before meeting - Update for meeting	- Impact on current production - Planned work for the next month	2 hours + 1 hour for Update
C Detail topics construction	Const-ruction super-visor	- 8 days before meeting - Update 3 days before meeting by mail	- Decision material for hall floor - Problem of contaminated soil	3 hours + 2 hours for Update
D Finance	Group Financial Officer	- 7 days before meeting - Update 2 days before meeting by mail	- Financial status - Costs in relation to construction progress - Cost compliance measures	3 hours + 2 hours for Update
E Decisions and next steps	Project manager	- In the meeting	- Summary of the de-cisions of the meeting	No preparation
Total time required				16 hours

Fig. 6.7 Current situation: facts for the preparation of the documents

2. The documents are prepared by different people depending on the topic. For the last meeting, the project manager, the construction supervisor and the group's financial manager independently prepared and sent out documents for the meeting. The project manager had the largest amount of work.
3. In terms of content, the various topics are not sufficiently coordinated. Although the parties involved regularly exchange information, there are still discrepancies because the documents are prepared at different times and various updates are made at short notice. This is the case, for example, with the calculation of the financial impact when choosing the material for the hall floor. The construction supervisor's calculations in topic C show a different value than the one used in the calculations regarding the financial status in topic D, which were made by the financial manager.
4. Requests for topics for the meeting are sometimes only communicated 4 days before the meeting in question. For example, the representative of the group wanted an analysis of the costs incurred in relation to the construction progress at short notice.

2. Determine fields of action

Based on the insights gained from recording the actual condition, the most important fields of action for optimising the current situation are then jointly determined. These are:

1. *Deadline for sending the documents:* Currently the deadline for sending the documents is 1 week before the meeting. This is very early and means that current topics and the latest developments are missing from the documents. This leads to subsequent revisions of the documents and additional mailing. The printouts of the documents and the additional delivery by post cause additional effort.
2. *Lack of coordination between stakeholders:* Mainly the project manager, the construction supervisor and the financial manager are involved in the preparation of the documents. Although there is a regular exchange between them, it is not directly related to the preparation of the documents for the project committee meeting. The preparation by different persons leads to duplications and results in several separate deliveries of the documents for the meeting.
3. *Topics are known too late:* Topics to be discussed at the project committee meeting are often determined at very short notice, although most of them have been known for some time. This leads to last-minute adjustments of the documents that have already been sent out and makes consultation between the participants more difficult.

3. Working on fields of action

Once the main fields of action have been identified, the next step is to work on them. In the process, approaches to improving the situation are developed together.

Field of action 1: Deadline for sending the documents

Figure 6.8 shows the result of the processing of field of action 1 'Deadline for sending the documents'. It is shown that by sending the documents electronically at a later date, the preparation effort can be greatly reduced. A large part of the short-term reworking and the resulting additional dispatch can be saved. Thanks to the electronic dispatch, printing and mailing are no longer necessary.

Field of action 2: Lack of coordination between stakeholders

The processing of this field of action shows that better coordination between the participants can greatly improve the quality of the documents. Therefore, it was

Points to improve	Solution approaches
➢ Printout and mailing cause great time expenditure.	➢ Documents are no longer printed. Dis-patch only takes place electronically.
➢ Sending the documents seven days before the meeting is very early.	➢ The final and complete documents are with the participants at least two days before the meeting.
Decision	**Expected impact**
Documents are to be sent to the participants by e-mail two days before the meeting.	Elimination of post-processing: time savings of four hours, since a large part of the post-processing as well as printing and shipping are eliminated.

Fig. 6.8 Field of action 1 'Deadline for sending the documents'

Points to improve	Solution approaches
➢ Currently, the documents are prepared by different persons.	➢ Someone takes the lead for creating and sending by e-mail.
➢ There is no coordination of the content of the different topics.	➢ Joint coordination of the content before sending the documents.
Decision	**Expected impact**
The project manager takes the lead for the creation and dispatch. A telephone coordination takes place before the dis-patch.	Slightly higher effort due to additional coordination of about one hour. But a strong improvement in the quality of the docu-ments.

Fig. 6.9 Field of action 2 'Lack of coordination between stakeholders'

Point to improve	Solution approaches
➢ Topics for the meeting are sometimes set at very short notice.	➢ At the end of the meeting, the topics for the next meeting are determined.
Decision	**Expected impact**
Topics are determined at the end of the previous meeting. Short-term topics can be reported to the project manager up to six days before the meeting.	Saving of two hours due to better planning, as early coordination is possible. In addition, the quality of the documents is increased.

Fig. 6.10 Field of action 3 'Topics are known too late'

decided to introduce, among other things, a telephone coordination before the submission of the documents. The findings from the processing of this field of action are summarised in Fig. 6.9.

Field of action 3: Topics are known too late

When working on field of action 3, it becomes apparent that the early determination of topics is crucial for an efficient and high-quality preparation of the documents. For this reason, the topics of the next project committee meeting should already be discussed and determined at the end of the previous meeting. Figure 6.10 shows the findings from the processing of this field of action.

4. Implement improvements

To sum up, the following measures for optimising the preparation of documents for the project committee are the result of the detailed processing of the individual fields of action:

1. For the last item of the project committee meeting, the topics for the next committee are determined. Urgent topics can be reported directly to the project leader up to 6 days before the meeting.

Topic of the workshop: Optimisation of the documents for the project committee	
Initial situation / problem description - The documents for the meeting do not meet the requirements and the coordi-nation in the preparation is poor. - The preparation of the documents takes too long and there are often subsequent adjustments.	Result - The current situation showed that the preparation of the documents took about 16 hours and that there was a lack of coordination. - Several fields of action for improvement could be identified and addressed.
Goal /Effect - Reduction of the time required to create the documents by 30%. - Preventing re-dispatch of documents. - Better coordination of the documents and therefore better quality of the contents.	Achieved effect and goals - Time required was reduced by over 30% (last creation took 11 hrs). - At the last meeting, no re-dispatch was necessary. - The participants perceive the quality of the documents to have greatly improved.

Fig. 6.11 One Pager on the topic of 'Optimisation of documents for the project committee'

2. The project leader takes the lead and coordinates the preparation of the documents. The other participants send their contributions to the project leader by e-mail at least 6 days before the meeting for integration into the overall presentation.
3. A conference call is held 3 days before the meeting to coordinate the documents. The project manager, the construction supervisor and the group's financial manager are involved. Depending on the topic, other people may be consulted.
4. The project manager now sends out the documents for the project committee meeting by e-mail 2 days before the meeting. The documents will no longer be printed out or sent by post.

The appointments for the coordination by phone are already scheduled during the workshop. For all other measures, the project manager takes responsibility for their implementation.

5. Check effect

At the next but one project committee meeting, a short review is conducted to check the effectiveness of the measures. The One Pager in Fig. 6.11 shows an overview of the results.

Practical Tips

1. Even in a situation where certain optimisations already seem obvious at the beginning of the workshop, it is very important that no steps are skipped in the processing. This prevents hasty measures from being taken and essential fields of action from being overlooked.
2. After the optimisations have been introduced, it is important to check their effectiveness and make adjustments if necessary.

6.1.3 Example 3: Optimising the Commenting of Internally Executed Projects

Muller Ltd. is part of a group of companies. The core competence of Muller Ltd. lies in the handling of transport services in Switzerland and nearby foreign countries. In addition to the actual transport services, the constant maintenance and modernisation of the company's own fleet of vehicles are also part of the main activities. To ensure the maintenance and modernisation of the vehicles, Muller Ltd. maintains several production plants at various locations in Switzerland. These production plants are organisationally combined in a separate business division. The organisational chart of Muller Ltd. is shown in Fig. 6.12.

The financial management of the current business is ensured independently by the Finance division of Muller Ltd. For the financial management of projects, however, the lead for all projects of the corporate group lies with the group's Finance. The organisation of Muller Ltd's Finance is structured as shown in Fig. 6.13.

In addition to ensuring all financial activities, Muller Ltd's Finance department also prepares the monthly reports on the course of business. The overlapping of the fields of work with regard to the financial management of the projects leads to duplications and coordination problems. This practical example for optimising work processes shows how the problem was tackled in the preparation of the reporting within the framework of an improvement workshop. The focus is on providing commentary on projects that were carried out in the company's own production plants.

Description of the Current Situation Before the Workshop

The following employees are involved in the commentaries on internally executed projects:

– John Fox: Head of Finance at Muller Ltd. and thus overall responsible for reporting at Muller Ltd.

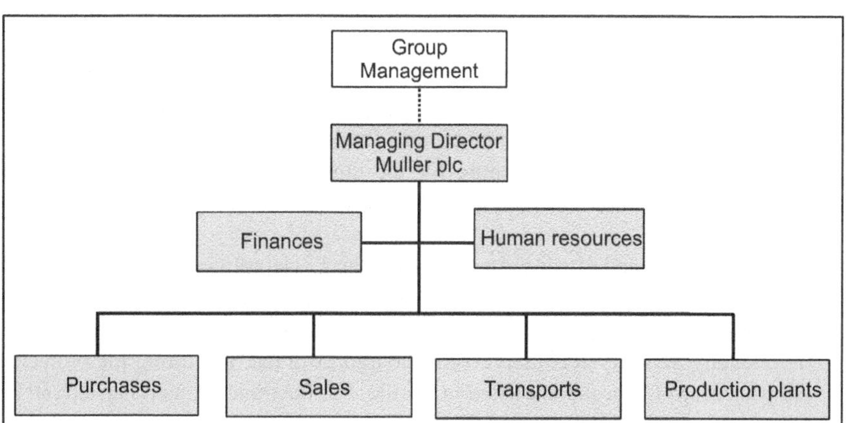

Fig. 6.12 Organisation Muller Ltd.

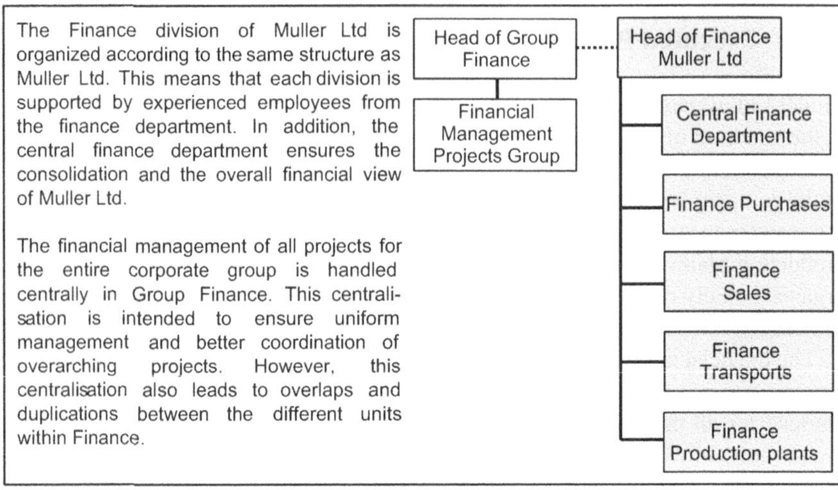

Fig. 6.13 Organisation of Finances at Muller Ltd.

- Sara Hill: Head of financial management of the group's projects
- Peter Morgan: Sara Hill's co-worker and financial manager for projects A and B
  - Project A involves the modernisation of 20 old Muller Ltd. trucks.
  - Project B involves retrofitting 25 trucks with new particle filters.
- Max Harris: Sara Hill's co-worker and financial manager for project C
  - Project C involves the modernisation of all forklifts at Muller Ltd.
- James Scott: Financial manager of the Muller Ltd. production plants
- The project leaders of projects A, B and C as input providers for the commentary on the respective projects
- The head of the production plants as input provider for the commentary on the works
- Tom Green: Central Finance Division of Muller Ltd., as recipient of the reporting

The individual activities of the main stakeholders for providing commentary on the monthly reporting are described in detail below.

Sara Hill, Head of Financial Management Projects Group

In her role, Sara Hill is responsible for the commentary on all projects of the corporate group. According to her role, she carries out the following activities:

1. After the month-end closing, she waits for the IT department to tell her that all figures have been entered into the system in full. This is usually the case 1 day after the closing. As soon as the data is uploaded, Sara Hill evaluates the projects individually in the system and records the figures in the 'Reporting file projects'. All projects of the group are listed in the file. For the three projects carried out by

Project	Target costs	Actual costs	Deviation	Comment
A				
B				
C				
D				
E				
F				
G				
H				
Total				

Fig. 6.14 Reporting file projects

Project	Target costs	Actual costs	Deviation	Comment
A				
B				
C				
Total				

Overall commentary projects executed by Muller Ltd

Fig. 6.15 Reporting file projects Muller Ltd.

Muller Ltd., it takes her a total of about 30 min to finish. The 'Reporting file projects' is structured as shown in Fig. 6.14.

2. Around noon of the first day after closing, she sends the evaluation to her staff members for comments (duration: 5 min).
3. In the course of the fourth day, she gets back the comments on the individual projects from her staff. She copies the comments on the three Muller Ltd. projects into the 'Reporting file projects Muller Ltd'. She also creates an overall commentary on these three projects. Inserting the data takes 10 min. The creation of the overall commentary takes another 30 min. The 'Reporting file projects Muller Ltd' is shown in Fig. 6.15.
4. She sends the file to James Scott, the financial manager of the production plants at Muller Ltd. (time required: 5 min).

Peter Morgan and Max Harris, Financial Managers of Projects A, B and C
The financial managers of the projects represent the financial division in the respective project committees. In this role, they know the current status and the planned progress of the respective projects. They are responsible for the commentary on the respective projects. Within the framework of the commentary, their activities are as follows:

1. After receiving the 'Reporting file projects' to comment on from their boss, they analyse the individual values. They use the accounting system to retrieve additional information (time required: 1 h per project).
2. They meet with the respective responsible project manager to discuss the project status and to jointly prepare the commentary. They complete these comments in the 'Reporting file projects' (time required: 1 h per project).
3. No later than the morning of the fourth day after the closing, Peter Morgan and Max Harris send the completed 'Reporting file projects' back to their boss by e-mail (duration: 5 min per employee).

James Scott, Financial Manager of the Production Plants
As the financial manager of the production plants, James Scott is responsible for the commentary on all the work in the production plants. His activities, within the framework of the commentary, are as follows:

1. After the IT department informs him that the data is correctly mapped in the system, he starts analysing all production orders and the cost centres in the system on the first working day after the closing (time required: 3 h).
2. He then transfers the data on the production plants from the system to the 'Reporting file production plants Muller Ltd' shown in Fig. 6.16. All costs incurred in the production plants are broken down into the cost categories 'personnel', 'material' and 'other costs'. The central finance department of Muller Ltd. has specified this structure for all divisions (time required: 30 min).
3. On the second day after the closing, he meets with the head of the production plants and discusses the monthly closing and the comments with him. The

Category	Target costs	Actual costs	Deviation	Comment
Personnel				
Material				
Other costs				
Total costs				

Fig. 6.16 Reporting file production plants Muller Ltd.

expenses for the projects carried out in the Muller Ltd. plants are discussed, but not entered into the 'Reporting file of the Muller Ltd. plants', as this is the responsibility of the financial managers of the projects. The meeting lasts about 2 h.

4. After receiving the list from Sara Hill, he transfers the comments on the projects to the 'Reporting file production plants Muller Ltd'. Since the breakdown of the costs by category is missing, he has to complete the allocation himself as best as possible in each case. In addition, he changes the comments on the projects according to his own assessment (duration 2 h 30 min).
5. At noon of the fourth working day at the latest, he sends the completed reporting file of the Muller Ltd. production plants to Tom Green of the central finance department (time required: 5 min).

Question

John Fox has heard from the employees involved in the commentary on the internally executed projects that they are not satisfied with the current situation. The employees complain that there are various duplications and that the effort required to prepare the reporting is very high. In addition, the deadline often cannot be met because the necessary information is passed on too late.

For this reason, John Fox contacts David Lee, the person responsible for improvements at Muller Ltd. He wants to clarify with him how the situation can be improved. Together they formulate the questions for the improvement project:

- How can the financial reporting of the projects executed by Muller Ltd. be prepared more efficiently? How can the existing duplications and coordination problems between the parties involved be reduced at the same time?

To address this issue, they want to hold an improvement workshop with all staff involved in the process.

Processing of the Improvement Project

Step 1: Create fact sheet and prepare workshop

In order to record the most important key points of the improvement project, Fritz Gerber and John Fox draw up the fact sheet shown in Fig. 6.17. On it, the initial situation with the expected goals and the delimitation of the focal points to be dealt with are determined. In addition, organisational points such as the determination of the participating employees and the time of implementation are recorded. For a detailed description of the tool 'fact sheet', see Sect. 4.1.2.

After John Fox has approved the fact sheet, Fritz Gerber begins to plan and prepare the implementation of the improvement workshop in detail. He lays out the procedure for working on the project as follows:

A. Discuss the initial situation.
B. Record the current situation.
C. Determine and prioritise fields of action.

Topic of the Workshops: Optimisation of commenting on internally executed projects	
Initial situation / problem description - Different views and different deadlines lead to duplications and contradictory comments.	Participants - Sara Hill: Head of Financial Management Projects Group - James Scott: production plants - Tom Green: Central Finance Department
Delimitation - The focus is on commenting on the projects carried out internally. - The focus is not on the cooperation with those responsible for the workshops in commenting.	Realisation Location: Zurich Date / Time: 20. + 21. May; 08:00 – 17:00 Final presentation: 16:30 – 17:00
Effect / Goal - Reduction of effort by 20% - Increase quality of comments - Increase in staff motivation	Signature sponsor: John Fox Head of Finance

Fig. 6.17 Fact sheet 'Optimisation of commenting on internally executed projects'

D. Work on fields of action.
E. Presentation of the new process.
F. Final presentation.

Step 2: Conduct of the workshop

The fact sheet and the planned schedule of the 2-day workshop are posted on the wall at the beginning as a clearly visible guideline for all participants. The following staff members are present: Fritz Gerber as improvement manager, Sara Hill as head of financial management of the group projects, her colleagues Peter Morgan and Max Harris as financial managers for the various projects, James Scott as financial manager for the production plants and Tom Green from the central finance department.

(A) Discuss the initial situation

The sponsor John Fox is also present at the opening of the improvement workshop. He opens the workshop by giving his view of the current situation and communicating his expectations to the staff involved. Afterwards, the issue and the fact sheet are discussed together.

(B) Record the current situation

In the first step, the current reporting process is recorded with a tool called 'Process Mapping' (a detailed description of the 'Process Mapping' can be found in Sect. 4.1.6). The result of the recording of the current situation is shown in Fig. 6.18.

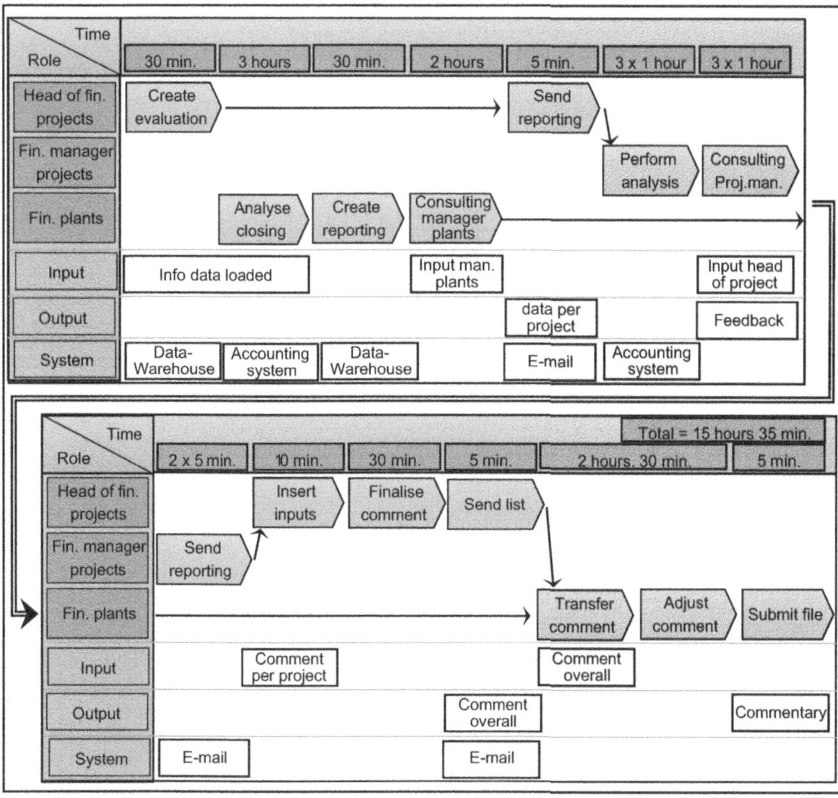

Fig. 6.18 Process Mapping of the current situation regarding the commentary on internally executed projects

(C) Determine and prioritise fields of action

After the completion of the recording of the current situation, the critical points of the process are marked together in the team. These are:

- *Different comment files:* The 'Reporting file projects Muller Ltd' and the 'Reporting file production plants Muller Ltd' have different structures. This leads to additional work when transferring the comments. In addition, there may be a loss of information because the comments are rewritten several times.
- *Time-consuming evaluation of the data:* The evaluation is not done by the financial managers of the projects, but by Sara Hill, the head of the financial management of the projects. This leads to an inefficient procedure with unnecessary amount of people involved.
- *Commenting on the projects takes place over several stages:* The commentary for the individual projects is prepared by the financial managers for the projects at the project level. Sara Hill, head of financial management of the projects, then prepares an overall commentary. This commentary is revised by James Scott,

Project	Target costs	Actual costs	Devia-tion	Comment by category	
A				Personnel	
				Material	
				Other costs	
B				Personnel	
				Material	
				Other costs	
C				Personnel	
				Material	
				Other costs	
Total				Personnel	
				Material	
				Other costs	

Fig. 6.19 Revised Reporting file Projects Muller Ltd.

the financial manager of the production plants, and transferred into a different structure.

– *Contact persons for queries are unclear:* The comments on the projects regularly lead to queries from Tom Green of the central finance department and from the production plants. Answering these questions is difficult for the financial managers of the projects because their original comments are changed several times. James Scott, for his part, knows the projects too little to be able to provide information himself. Answering the questions regularly leads to duplication and additional time is required. About 2 h per month are spent on this.

(D) Work on fields of action

For each of the four fields of action, suggestions for optimisation are developed in the workshop. These are:

Field of action 1: Different comment files

The financial managers of the projects enter the comments directly into the 'Reporting file project Muller Ltd'. This reporting file is expanded as shown in Fig. 6.19 to ensure the same depth of commentary everywhere.

Field of action 2: Time-consuming evaluation of the data

Until now, Sara Hill has been inserting the latest data for commenting into the 'Reporting file projects'. She then sends this file to her employees. Now the data for the Muller Ltd. projects are loaded from the system by one of the two employees and entered into the adapted 'Reporting file projects Muller Ltd'. The overall commentary of the projects for Muller Ltd. is now also created by one of the financial managers of the projects. This reduces Sara Hill's workload as well as the number of interfaces.

The file is sent directly to James Scott by one of the financial managers of the projects. Sara Hill receives the 'Reporting file projects Muller Ltd' for information.

Field of action 3: Commenting on the projects takes place over several stages
So far, James Scott has been adjusting the comments on the projects and transferring them to the document 'Reporting file production plants Muller Ltd'. In the workshop, it was jointly decided that the lead for the commentary on the projects now lies with the financial managers of the projects. This means that James Scott takes over the comments and no longer adjusts them. With the added comments by category, it is possible for him to finish his work quickly in the future. In addition, James Scott will no longer analyse the production orders of the projects, as these are already analysed in detail by the financial managers of the projects (time saving of 1 h).

Field of action 4: Contact persons for queries are unclear
In the workshop, it is jointly decided that all questions concerning the internally executed projects will be conveyed directly to the financial managers of the projects. James Scott is responsible for all other financial questions concerning the production plants.

(E) Presentation of the new process
After working on the fields of action, the target process flow is drawn, taking into account the improvement measures. Figure 6.20 shows the target Process Mapping.

The newly created target process has obviously been streamlined. By handing over her activities to her staff, Sara Hill is no longer actively involved in the commentary. This eliminates interfaces and duplications. In addition, the process is considerably faster because James Scott no longer has to adjust the comments on the projects.

(F) Final presentation
At the end of the workshop, the participants present the findings and results to all interested stakeholders. Among others, the managing director of Muller Ltd., the head of the production plants and several employees of the finance department are in attendance at this presentation. In particular, the clear allocation of responsibilities for queries about the projects and the improved quality of the comments are acknowledged as positive progress.

After the Workshop

Two months after the workshop, all participants meet again for a short review. This is to check whether the measures taken have had the desired effect and whether the process is being lived according to the new guidelines.

The feedback from the participants is consistently positive. Thanks to the streamlined process, the workload is less than before and the time pressure has decreased noticeably. In addition, the quality of the comments has been greatly improved, as they are no longer changed several times by different staff members. As a result, there are fewer queries, and the time spent on them has been reduced by half.

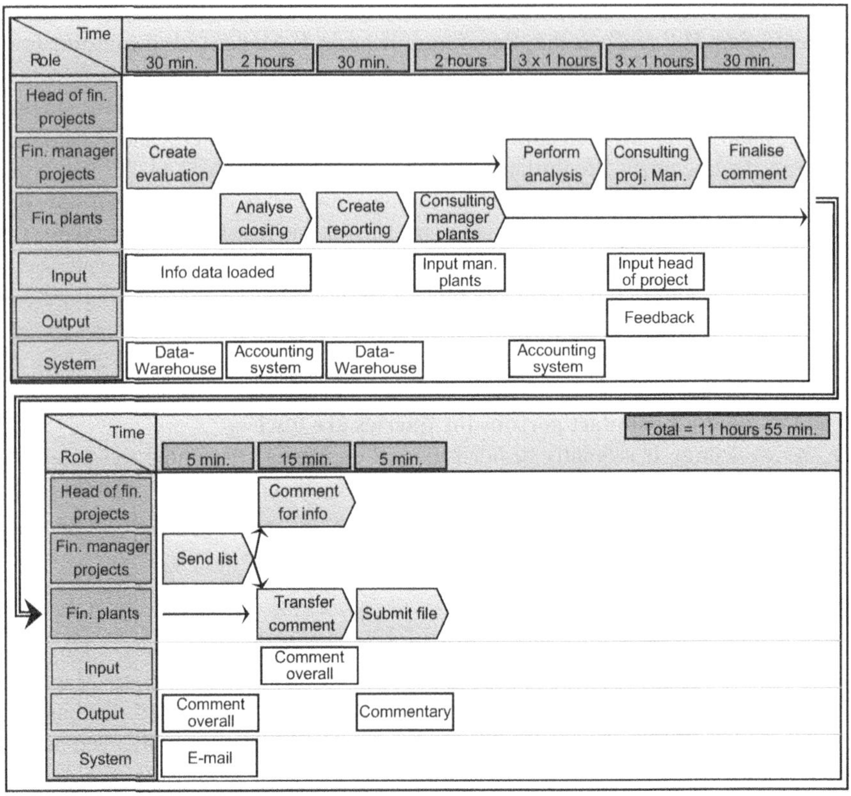

Fig. 6.20 Target Process Mapping of commenting on internally executed projects

The result of the review is recorded in a One Pager. (For a description of the One Pager, see Sect. 4.1.15). Figure 6.21 shows the One Pager created for this improvement project.

Practical Tips

1. Especially with more complex issues, a short preliminary discussion with the employees involved is useful. The discussion helps to inform the employees about the workshop and to collect their expectations.
2. To check the measures taken, it is advisable to simulate the new target process during the workshop. In this example, the revised 'Reporting file projects Muller Ltd' is passed on from participant to participant. The activities that arise according to the new target process are simulated in order to test whether the structure of the file meets the requirements of the participants.

Topic of the Workshops: Optimisation of commenting on internally executed projects

Initial situation / problem description	Result
- Different views and different deadlines lead to duplications and contradictory comments.	- Standardisation of comment files. - Establishment of clear responsibilities. - Process documentation is updated in the system.
Goal / Effect	**Achieved effect and goals**
- Reduction of effort by 20%. - Increase quality of comments. - Increase in staff motivation.	- Reduction of effort by 23%. - Clear improvement in quality leads to fewer queries and more time savings. - Positive feedback from all participants.

Fig. 6.21 One Pager on the result of the improvement project 'Optimisation of commenting on internally executed projects'

6.2 Practical Experience of an Expert on the Kaizen Method

Putting theoretical principles into practice is often more difficult than expected, and only with several years of experience from many improvement projects can the full potential be used. One person who can confirm this from personal experience is Stephan Spada. He has been conducting workshops according to the Kaizen method at the Swiss Federal Railways (SBB) for more than 10 years and also deals intensively with the topic of improvement management as a lecturer at renowned schools and professional symposia.

Stephan Spada is a Kaizen Project Manager at the Swiss Federal Railways (SBB) Infrastructure and co-responsible for the introduction of Kaizen Office (Administration). After studying tourism at the University of Applied Sciences Kempten and at the University of Angers ESTHUA (France), he was Head of Quality, Service and Processes at the premium night train company CityNightLine. In 2002, he moved to the SBB, where he has accompanied and co-managed the introduction of Kaizen in passenger transport sales since 2008. In 2014, he won the German and American Idea Award, as well as the Best Trainee Idea Award in 2015, 2017 and 2018. Since 2010, more than 80 large Kaizen process optimisation workshops have been conducted, and the Kaizen Office methods have been continuously developed in a practice-oriented manner on the basis of 10 diploma theses.

In the following interview, he talks about his experiences with the Kaizen method in everyday life and gives helpful advice when working with the application of the Kaizen philosophy.

6.2.1 Interview with Stephan Spada

How Did You First Get Involved in the Topic of Process Improvement?
At the beginning of 2008, Kaizen Agents were sought in the sales department of the SBB Passenger Transport with a commitment of 20%, within the traditional field of activity, to support the introduction of Kaizen. As I have always been fascinated by improvement management (implementing ideas at work), I immediately applied. We introduced Kaizen the classic way: first, in 2009, optimising the workplace with the help of the 5S method, then improving teamwork and, in 2010, holding the first process improvement workshops with topics that were optimised across departments.

What Fascinates You About This Topic and Your Work?
As a Kaizen manager, you will always come into contact with new improvement topics. The work is very varied and requires a wide range of different skills: good comprehension and linking of contexts, psychological empathy towards the participants of a Kaizen activity (e.g. in case of their lack of motivation or understanding of a topic), language skills, perseverance, etc.

What Framework Conditions Must Be Met in a Company in Order to Be Able to Establish Successful Improvement Management?
By introducing the success formula (ambition, responsibility, trust and room for manoeuvre), the SBB has created an important basis for the successful introduction of Kaizen. This enables employees to proactively and independently implement improvement measures in their environment for the benefit of customers. This increases staff motivation and strengthens the connection of the employees to the company in the long term.

Why Do You Use the Kaizen Method for the Most Part?
I like the intrinsic approach: Only when employees and managers understand and internalise Kaizen as a philosophy/attitude, they are ready to successfully implement Kaizen activities. Kaizen is therefore not a doctrine that comes from the management, but a bottom-up approach. Since the involvement of employees in Kaizen activities is essential and the solutions developed are tested immediately, the likelihood of solutions disappearing unused and without added value after a short time is reduced.

Where Do You See the Difference to Other Methods?
Kaizen, unlike innovation, for example, is incremental and continuously repeated improvement in small steps. In this way, many small improvement measures can also result in a large leap in productivity. Agile and Kaizen are based on the same principles, whereby Agile is mostly used in the development of new products and Kaizen is applied in the optimisation of rule-based, repetitive and already existing processes.

What Is Particularly Important to Consider When Preparing a Kaizen Workshop?
The topic must be specified with the client in such a way that there is no room for interpretation for the participants as to which aspects are covered and which are not. In addition, it must be checked whether the topic can be dealt with using Kaizen. If it is about the costly optimisation of an IT programme, Kaizen is not the right approach. Furthermore, the Kaizen methodology that provides the greatest benefit with the least effort should be chosen.

What Are the Biggest Challenges for You When Conducting a Workshop?
Spontaneous changes, such as an important participant dropping out, or the framework conditions of the topic changing by incorporating new aspects not yet considered into the topic, which in turn trigger preparatory work. From my point of view, flexibility is one of the most important success factors for Kaizen.

What Tools Do You Use Regularly in Your Workshops?
For simple problems that can be localised in a team, we use the improvement story. This makes it possible to arrive at a solution with the employees concerned within about 1 h, including the determination of concrete measures.

For problems that affect several divisions working together on the basis of a process, the Kaizen workshop with the following procedure is the ideal tool:

1. Drawing up the Process Mapping (Value Stream Analysis of the current and lived process) and determining the problems.
2. Outlining the ideal state.
3. Reduction or elimination of problems that bring the current process closest to the ideal state.
4. The development of the target process (Value Stream Design). The Kaizen workshop tool can be supplemented and supported by other Kaizen tools, such as the Activity Analysis, Order Analysis or Information Structure Analysis.

And Which One of These Is Your Favourite Tool?
In my last position as a Kaizen manager for the sales department of the SBB Passenger Transport, we devised, tested and continuously developed the improvement story in the Kaizen team. I regularly use this in Kaizen workshops to reduce/eliminate prioritised problems.

Can You Briefly Describe the Improvement Story?
The improvement story is a predefined process that enables a structured handling of improvement projects. The implementation takes place in six steps, which are mapped accordingly in the following fields:

In the first field (Description of Problem (Deviation)/Waste/Ambition), it is important to briefly describe the initial situation so that it is clear what is and what is not covered in the improvement story. Keywords can be used to speed up the flow of information. If there are several problems in the initial situation, they can be prioritised by the participants in the improvement story. Basic rule: Always start with only one problem.

In the second field (Objectives), the objectives are to be defined within the framework of the possibilities according to the SMART formula. The term 'SMART' stands for the following abbreviations: 'Specific', 'Measurable', 'Attainable', 'Relevant' and 'Time-bound'. It is recommended to formulate quantitative and qualitative goals.

In the third field (Causes), the causes for the initial situation are elicited in a differentiated way. It is recommended to use the *Ishikawa Diagram* in order to find as many causes as possible and to use the *5 Whys technique* in order to understand the origin of individual causes in more depth. The identified causes are prioritised again, and the cause that most strongly triggers the initial situation is transferred to the fourth field.

In the fourth field (Solution Search), we recommend using a mind map when searching for solutions. Insert the prioritised cause in the middle and briefly describe and number the possible solutions all around. Then position the numbers in the four quadrants of the cost-benefit diagram so that the solution approach with the least cost for implementation and the greatest benefit emerges.

The fifth field (Measures) describes the measures (what, when, who) that are necessary to realise the solution.

In the sixth and last field (Impact Monitoring, Standardisation, Further Communication), impact monitoring is carried out after the passing of a defined time frame: The actually achieved solutions are compared with the defined goals. Where is there still a need for action? Can the measures be implemented in the next improvement story with even less effort? The question of whether a new standard can be derived from the solution (locally/regionally/Switzerland-wide) must also be clarified.

Finally, do not forget to communicate the successfully implemented improvement story as best practice so that other areas can also benefit from the solution.

What Needs to Be Taken into Account So That the Improvements Made Can Be Implemented in Everyday Life?

When determining measures to implement the solution, it is important to ensure that only participants who take part in the workshop can be designated as responsible. If employees are involved without their knowledge, it often happens that they cannot implement the measures because they do not have the time, for instance. It is also essential that participants meet regularly after the workshop to review the progress in implementing the measures and to make further improvements to the measures if necessary (PDCA cycle).

What Appeals to You About Improvement Management?

For me, improvement management is generally an easy and successful methodology to apply. So, we also apply it regularly at home, for example, in optimising the household or in dealing efficiently and effectively with the homework of our children.

Do You Have Any Further Experience with Improvement Management?
Since around 2014, I have had a lecturing mandate at my former university in France (ESTHUA de l'Université d'Angers) for master students to pass on theoretical and practical knowledge of Kaizen to them as part of their hotel, restaurant and event management studies. The lecture is partly carried out in collaboration with the Head of Quality Management/Kaizen of *SNCF Voyages*. I have also been able to give several Kaizen lectures in business studies at the University of Applied Sciences in Bern.

Where Are the Differences in Teaching to Implementation in Practice?
My teaching of Kaizen lectures to students at the University of Angers *(ESTHUA)* is a mixture of theory and practice. It is important that the students are enabled to apply the Kaizen methodology in practice themselves. First, for example, the process of an improvement story is explained to the students. Then they apply it themselves with a concrete practical example, such as: How can the proportion of food that is subsequently discarded be reduced at a breakfast buffet in a luxury hotel?

At an SBB Kaizen workshop, in contrast to the studies, the participants are not empowered and therefore only very briefly introduced to the theory, as a Kaizen coach is available for the implementation (facilitation).

Thank you very much for the interview. Can you give us a concrete example of how a Kaizen workshop proceeds for you?
First of all, the initial situation, the goals and the participants are recorded in the document 'Kaizen Workshop Dossier' (KWS Dossier) in collaboration with the client. As for the initial situation, it is important to determine which aspects will be dealt with and which will not be dealt with in order to avoid misunderstandings among the participants. This delineation of aspects is shown in an In-Frame and Out-of-Frame grid.

As an example of the process of optimisation with the Kaizen method, I can show the following improvement project from the financial sector of the SBB infrastructure:

6.2.2 Practical Example by Stephan Spada: 'Current Process IT Controlling'

In December 2018, we optimised the IT controlling process on behalf of Finance Infrastructure as part of a Kaizen process improvement workshop. All IT projects of Infrastructure above a defined volume have to go through this process. This process is very well suited for the application of the Kaizen methodology, as a large number of roles from different areas are involved, which carry out a variety of activities. This results in many interfaces between the roles, and the regulatory effort is considerable.

Area:	...	Topic:	Optimisation of IT controlling processes	Priority:	1

Initial situation	Procedure	Impact
All IT infrastructure projects above a defined volume have to go through this process. A large number of roles from different areas are involved in this process, which carry out a variety of activities. This results in many interfaces between the roles, and the regulatory effort is considerable.	Workshop for process participants in IT controlling: • 03.12. Recording of actual process / improvement story • 04.12. Improvement story / optimised current process measures and responsibilities Before the workshop, an activity analysis of the employees of the IT controlling process was carried out over approx. four weeks.	– Improve quality – Increase employee satisfaction – Acceleration of processing of delivery objects **Critical points** - Consideration of change in the approval process (start of new process in 2019).
Goal (objective + qualitative)	**Team**	**Dates**
The following goals are to be achieved by the end of the first quarter of 2019: • Elaboration / Harmonisation of the process. • Clarification of whether the resource structure of IT controlling is sufficient. • Optimisation of the current basic process.	Participants: – Head of IT Controlling – IT controlling staff Selective: – Employee IT Portfolio Management – Head of Project Accounting Finance – Head of committee FBP (Financial Business Partner) – Line representative in FBP – Employee IT Business Control	- Training Kaizen 10.10.2018 - Preparation Workshop 10/2018 - Implementation Kaizen activity 12/2018 (1.5 days) - Implementation of measures from January 2019 - 1st PDCA quality cycle with all employees of the workshop beginning of April 2019 **Sponsor** – Head of IT Controlling

Fig. 6.22 Kaizen workshop fact sheet 'Optimisation of IT controlling processes' (Source: Stephan Spada)

In order to optimise the process with the least possible effort and the greatest possible added value for the infrastructure, the first step is for the Kaizen coach and the client to complete the fact sheet. This is shown in Fig. 6.22.

When filling in the form, it is important that all relevant stakeholders are consulted for the process. If a stakeholder is not properly consulted or is forgotten, there is a risk that the result of the workshop cannot be fully implemented afterwards, for example, because the stakeholder does not release the resources of his employees to implement the measures defined in the workshop.

In the initial situation, it is sufficient to describe the problem and the deviations from a standard or challenge in a few sentences. If possible, the goals should always be formulated in SMART terms. In the process, the methodical approach is determined: which Kaizen tools are appropriate to be able to achieve the goals. When determining the team for the workshop, it is important to take into account that the people who work with the process constantly are invited, so that they have the necessary practical experience to determine the correct and effective improvements afterwards. The impact section shows which of the nine SBB corporate goals are affected by the outcome of the Kaizen workshop. Particular attention should be paid to the area of critical points/areas of caution: For example, has there already been a Kaizen workshop on this topic? How were the results introduced? Can the experience gained back then be incorporated into the new Kaizen workshop? Have any technological hurdles arisen?

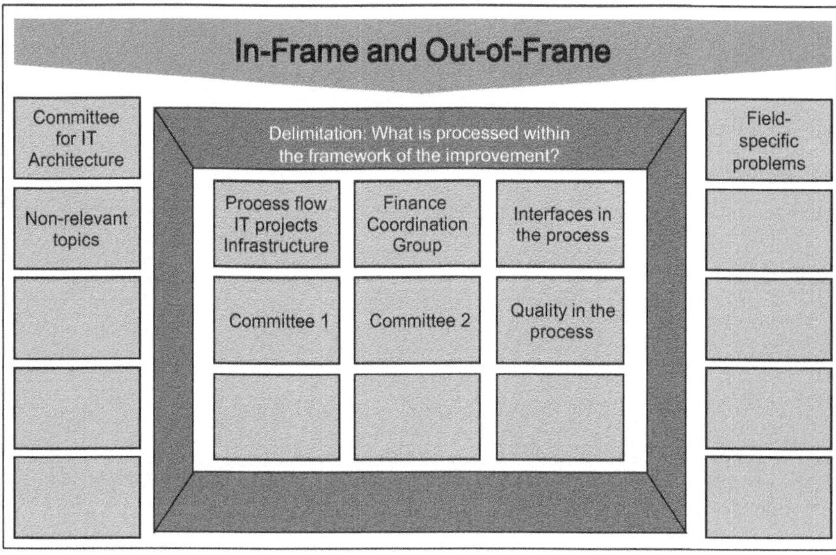

Fig. 6.23 In-Frame and Out-of-Frame optimisation process IT controlling (Source: Stephan Spada)

It is essential that the client (technical lead) and the Kaizen coach (methodological lead) are two different roles. Otherwise, there is a danger that the Kaizen coach will give technical instructions that do not correspond to the line's ideas.

It is important to determine before the workshop which topics are to be dealt with and which are not to be dealt with during the workshop. This delimitation must be agreed upon with all stakeholders and stakeholder groups so that there is a uniform understanding. This sounds simple in theory, but in practice, it can be very demanding to place all expectations and wishes of the stakeholders accordingly without jeopardising the implementation of the workshop with the chosen Kaizen method. A tip here: Allow enough time for this step. Not all stakeholders are available at all times, or they may need time to get an idea of the workshop. Figure 6.23 shows the delimitation of the improvement project to the topic 'Optimisation of IT controlling'.

One afternoon, in collaboration with the client, who is also responsible for the process in the role of process owner, and the employees concerned, who regularly work with the process, we visualised the actual process on brown paper: 16 roles (blue sticky notes) carry out 47 activities (yellow sticky notes), whereby not all roles are equally actively involved in the process. Thirteen roles are occupied by Infrastructure, one by Finance Corporate, one by the Shared Service Centre Finance and one by SBB IT. A central element in the process is a committee that reviews and approves the IT projects after each completed phase. This is done on the basis of a large number of documents to be submitted, such as the controlling report or the reporting files. At the end of the assessment of the current situation, the items in the process that show potential for improvement are marked with a red sticky note. Two

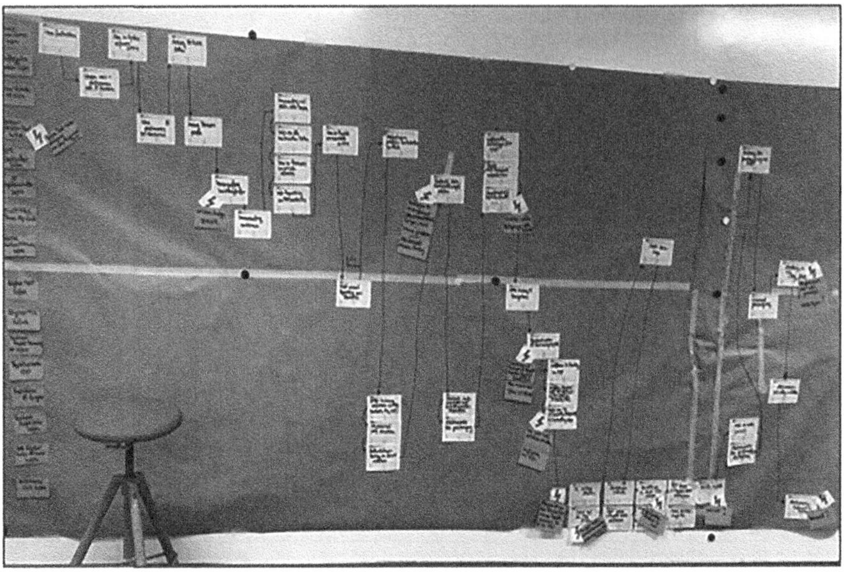

Fig. 6.24 Current Process Mapping IT controlling (Source: Stephan Spada)

fields of action were identified: There is no tool support in the process, which means that all information and documents are sent via e-mail, resulting in downstream roles in the process having no overview of what upstream roles have exchanged in terms of information. In addition, there is no process documentation (instructions), with the effect that the roles involved in the process carry out the stipulated tasks and activities differently. This creates a ping-pong and results in delays in the activities. The lead time of the process is prolonged.

Tip: If possible, roughly record the current process with the people concerned in advance in order to reduce the time for recording the current situation at the workshop to a minimum. This is particularly relevant for processes with many roles, as otherwise the employees will get bored if they have entered their activities in 5 minutes in the afternoon and the other employees spend the rest of the time describing their tasks. Figure 6.24 shows the result of recording the current state of IT controlling on the brown paper.

The lightning bolts on the current Process Mapping were prioritised by the workshop participants. Two working groups then developed specific solutions. These were subsequently coordinated in the plenary, consolidated and entered into a common list of measures. The complete overview of all measures developed in the workshop to optimise IT controlling is shown in Fig. 6.25.

Some of the measures listed are described in more detail here:

Explanation of the Measure to Document the Process

In order to achieve a uniform level of knowledge among those involved in the process, the process is documented with all its tasks. Each task has a defined input

No	What	who	when
1	Documentation of the IT controlling process	Employees finance Business Management	end Q1.2019
2	Setting up a workflow	Employees finance Business Management	end Q1.2019
3	Training of process stakeholders: 1. Financial templates 2. Process	1. Head IT-Controlling 2. Employees finance Business Management	end Q2.2019
4	Define information recipient at start of project / phase opening for Finance Shared Service Centre	Employees finance Business management	end Jan. 2019
5	Mapping projects in SAP	Employees finance Shared Service Centre	end Q1.2019

Fig. 6.25 List of measures for optimising the IT controlling process (Source: Stephan Spada)

and output. In order to be able to answer any questions about the process professionally, a specialist user support will be set up as a single point of contact. Currently, questions are received at various points in the process with the risk that these do not have sufficient resources to answer them.

Explanation of the Measure to Set Up a Workflow

The optimised current process was defined with the approach that a workflow is set up. This means that the downstream process step can only be started when the previous step has been completed.

Explanation of the Measure to Train the Process Stakeholders

As soon as the measure for documenting the process is completed, the people concerned with the process are trained. This can be used to check whether the documentation is comprehensible to them and whether they see further opportunities for improvement.

In order to make the status of the implementation of the measures clear, they have been recorded in a planner (Office 365 tool from Microsoft) with the following criteria:

- Status: Not started, in progress, done
- Assign to
- Due date
- Description
- Attachment (if available)
- Comments

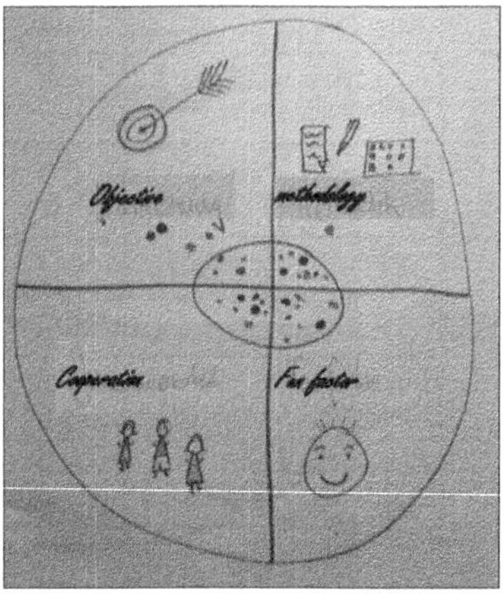

Summary

- The methodological approach, the cooperation and the fun factor were positively highlighted.
- The dots outside the achievement of objectives refer to the only partially fulfilled expectations that Quick Wins can be implemented in a timely manner.
- In the medium term, noticeable improvements in the IT controlling process can be realised after the implementation of the measures.
- Short-term improvements have been defined.
- Determination of information recipients at the start of the project / phase.
- Preparation of documentation and manuals as well as training of those involved in the process.
- A follow-up workshop is planned for the beginning of 2019.

Fig. 6.26 Participants' feedback optimisation IT controlling (Source: Stephan Spada)

Review of the Workshop

In order to continuously monitor the implementation of the measures, meetings (quality circles or PDCA meetings) of 1 h with the following objectives have been scheduled with all participants of the workshop at intervals of 2–3 months in order to check:

- Whether and how the measures have been implemented
- Whether there are further possibilities for improvement
- Whether obstacles to implementation have arisen that need to be resolved
- Whether interdependencies between the measures to be implemented need to be taken into account
- Whether synergies between the measures to be implemented can be used

Figure 6.26 shows the participants' feedback at the end of the Kaizen workshop. This is very important for measuring the satisfaction of the employees involved in the workshop. It is the basis for further improving the next procedure of a Kaizen workshop from the lessons learned (reduction of effort for preparation, implementation and follow-up of the workshop versus increase of benefit for the client). Standing still in the methodology means going backwards. It is important that the participants of the workshop receive feedback on their inputs by a defined point in time. Otherwise, this can be very frustrating for the participants of the workshop, and they will not give any more feedback on further Kaizen activities.

A Kaizen workshop is only a milestone in continuous improvement. In order to implement improvement sustainably in practice and to carry it out on a recurring basis, it must be regularly integrated into everyday work so that it is no longer perceived as a separate and isolated activity.

Practical Tips

1. Define the workshop topic precisely. Otherwise, there is a risk of endless discussions in the workshop.
2. Determine the flight level when recording the lived current process in order to avoid conflicts arising during the workshop due to the different expectations of the participants and to ensure that the set goals can also be achieved.
3. The workshop does not end with the catalogue of measures. The follow-up of the implementation of the measures and their possible further improvement are just as fundamental as conducting the workshop itself.

Simulations to Illustrate the Improvement Methods

7

Simulations to Illustrate the Improvement Methods
By means of short simulations, the key points of the improvement methods can be communicated clearly and efficiently. The employees involved actively shape the process and experience the resulting improvements, which leads to a positive learning effect. The examples presented in this chapter are very well suited for inclusion in improvement workshops or to lighten up seminars and training events.

M. Hofmann, *A Holistic Approach to Process Optimisation*, Management for Professionals, https://doi.org/10.1007/978-3-658-34097-1_7

7.1 Simulations to Illustrate the Improvement Methods

Simulations in the context of improvement management are practical exercises that represent a simple and efficient way of conveying the contents and philosophies of the various improvement methods. It is particularly advantageous that the employees involved work on the tasks themselves. This enables the active design and direct experience of the changes and leads to a lasting experience and a corresponding learning effect. The simulations presented here are carried out in small groups. This additionally promotes cooperation and team building.

Simulations to optimise work processes can be used in different situations. They are particularly well suited for use in the following situations:

A. To support theoretical training on improvement management
B. At team events for team building
C. To loosen up in seminars

In detail, these situations are described here:

(A) To support theoretical training on improvement management
In training courses, it is generally important to support the theoretical teaching of the material by incorporating practical tasks and exercises. This is no different for training in the context of improvement management. The following goals can be achieved by incorporating simulations:

- Loosening up the lessons
- Actively experiencing the philosophy and impact of the improvement methods
- Greater learning effect
- Sustainable anchoring of the substance

(B) At team events for team building
The improvement methods rely heavily on the involvement of the employees concerned and on optimisation in the team. The simulations described support this basic idea in that the processing or at least the final analysis takes place in groups. Thus, the simulations described are also excellent for team building.

The simulations can be easily incorporated into team workshops or at a joint event and help to improve cooperation in teams.

(C) To loosen up in seminars
Long lectures and elaborate speeches often lead to seminars being perceived as a rather dry affair and participants tend to get bored. This can be prevented by incorporating short simulations to activate the participants.

At the same time, these short interactive sequences promote contact between the participants. Thus, people who normally hardly work together exchange ideas and get to know each other better.

Several examples of simple simulations for everyday use are described on the following pages.

7.1.1 Simulation 1: Standardisation

This simulation serves to illustrate the benefits of standardisation and the 5S approach from the Kaizen method (Fig. 7.1) (for a detailed description, see Sect. 3.1.2).

Possible Applications/Benefits

This short and simple simulation can be easily integrated into training sessions. It convincingly conveys to the participants the advantages of a standardised procedure when performing recurring activities and promotes the discussion on standardisation in the group.

Carrying Out the Simulation

Preparation

Four different sheets with different levels of standardisation are to be drawn up for each participant. The individual sheets are to be prepared as follows (see Figs. 7.2 and 7.3).

- Sheet 1: This sheet represents the initial situation. It contains a disorderly jumble of numbers and letters in different formatting. Except for the number 18, all numbers from 1 to 24 are present on the sheet.

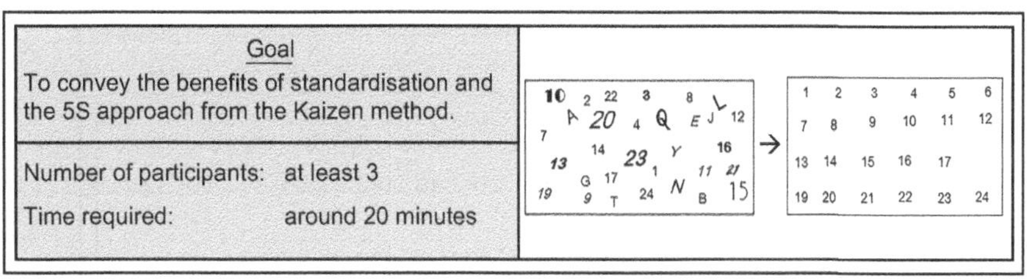

Fig. 7.1 Simulation for standardisation

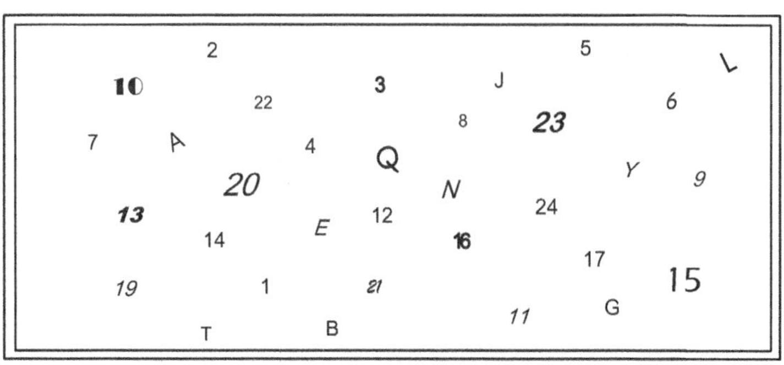

Fig. 7.2 Simulation template for standardisation—sheet 1

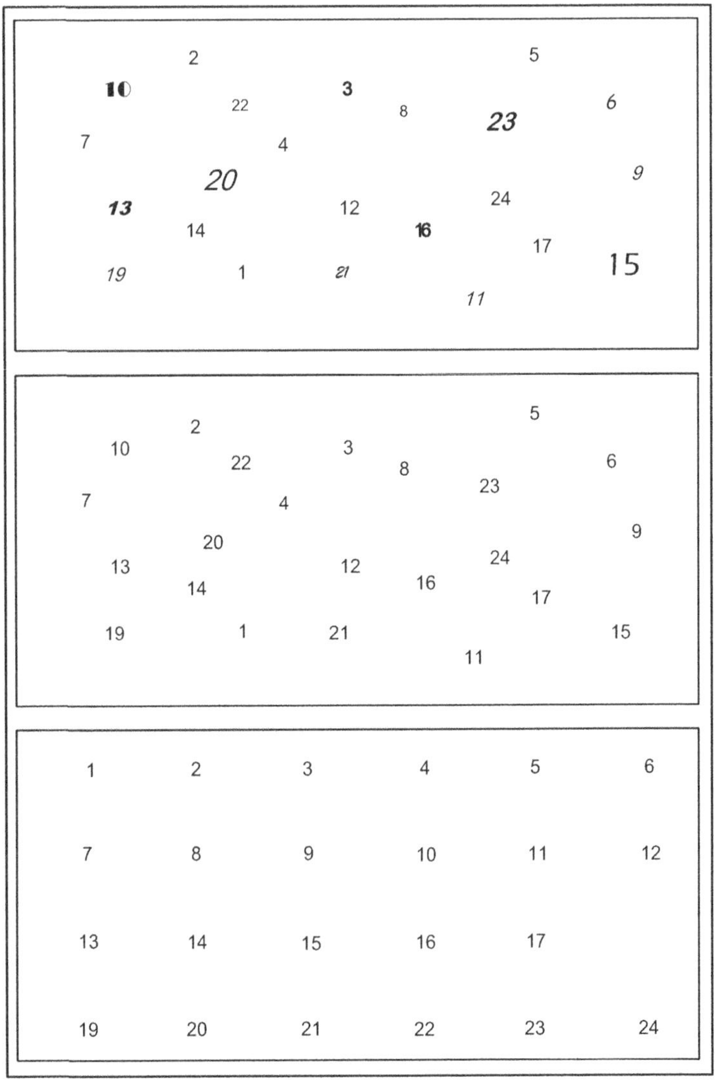

Fig. 7.3 Simulation template for standardisation—sheets 2–4

- Sheet 2: This sheet shows the situation after all the letters have been combed out. It matches sheet 1 but without the letters.
- Sheet 3: This sheet represents the situation after cleaning the numbers. For this purpose, all existing numbers are shown in the same format.
- Sheet 4: The last sheet represents the situation after having put the numbers in order. For this purpose, the existing numbers are listed one after the other. The space for the number 18 remains empty.

Procedure

1. To introduce the simulation, the facilitator explains to the participants the initial situation and the rules to be considered. These are as follows:
   - Each participant receives a sheet of paper with jumbled numbers and letters. Their task is to connect the numbers from 1 to 24 with a continuous line as quickly as possible.
   - Note that one number is missing. This number is to be skipped and noted at the top of the sheet.
   - The first person to connect all the numbers calls out 'stop' and names the missing number.
2. The first sheet, which contains both numbers and letters, is placed face down on the table in front of the participants. At the facilitator's signal, the participants turn over the sheet and start completing the task. With the start signal, the time is started.
3. As soon as the first participant has connected all the numbers and correctly named the missing number, the time is stopped. The time is noted on the board as attempt 1.
4. The same procedure is repeated next with the second sheet. The fastest time is written on the board as attempt 2.
5. One after the other, the task is repeated for sheets 3 and 4. Here, too, the times are written on the board.

Evaluation

After the task has been completed for all four sheets, the times of the four attempts are compared and reflected on in the group. The participants should answer the following two questions:

- What insights did they gain from the simulation carried out?
- What conclusions can be drawn from this for your daily work? Do you have any concrete examples?

Even though this simulation actually consists of individual work, the subsequent discussion in the group contributes to the team building and to improving cooperation. The discussion on concrete examples from the participants' everyday lives often turns out to be particularly interesting.

> **Practical Tips**
> 1. Leave enough time for the participants to reflect on the results at the end. Especially the question about concrete examples from practice can trigger very interesting and insightful discussions.
> 2. This simulation can also be performed as group work. In this case, groups of three to four participants are formed. The initial situation and the rules remain unchanged. It is interesting to observe how the group organises itself to be able to solve the task as quickly as possible and who takes on which role within the group.

7.1.2 Simulation 2: Simulation with Building Blocks

This simulation is suitable for gathering practical experience with optimising processes in teams. Starting from the current process, which is available here in the form of a construction manual, the assembly of a vehicle is to be optimised. For this simulation, for example, simple LEGO® construction kits or similar models of other makes available on the market are suitable. It is important to have a sufficient number of components (more than 60). Otherwise, the assembly is too simple and does not offer sufficient possibilities for improvement (Fig. 7.4).

Possible Applications/Benefits

This practical exercise is ideal for use in both improvement management training and team building. The participants apply the procedure for continuous improvement and further development of processes in a simple way. Furthermore, they learn to recognise waste and to reduce or eliminate it. At the same time, teamwork is strengthened and promoted. My observations during the utilisation of the simulation have shown that a lively discussion takes place in the groups and that waste in the process is quickly recognised and eliminated. This experience always leads to exciting insights in the final discussion when it comes to the question of the benefits of improvement management for everyday life.

In principle, the simulation can already be carried out with a group of three to four participants. However, it is more exciting if at least two to three different groups compete against each other.

Carrying Out the Simulation

Preparation

Before conducting the simulation, the following tools are to be organised:

- One construction kit per group for assembly. For comparability of the results, it is necessary that all groups receive the same construction kit. When choosing the construction kit, make sure that it can be assembled in about 5 minutes.
- A stopwatch to measure time.
- Flipchart and pens for the evaluation part.

Goal	
Optimising a simple team process and identifying waste.	
Number of participants:	3 - 4 perteam; plus possibly 1 observer
Time required:	about 1 hour

Fig. 7.4 Simulation with building blocks

Procedure

The simulation proceeds as follows:

1. The participants are divided into groups of three to four people. It is advantageous to form groups that are as heterogeneous as possible and have not worked together before in order to be able to generate the improvement ideas from many different perspectives.
2. The facilitator introduces the initial situation and the task according to the description in Fig. 7.5. Ideally, this description is pinned to the wall for all participants to see.
3. The teams start with the first assembly according to the assembly instructions enclosed. As soon as the first team has finished, the time is written down. The other teams may still finish building their model and also write down their time.
4. The first round is reflected on in the teams and optimisations are developed. The following questions should be answered and written down on a flipchart:
   - Recording of the current process
   - Pointing out the difficulties and wastes discovered in the current process by using the symbol of a lightning bolt
   - Determining causes why the difficulties occurred
   - Outlining the ideal process
   - Prioritisation of the difficulties whose reduction/elimination brings the team closest to the ideal process
   - Working out improvements to the difficulties discovered
   - Determining the target process
5. Another assembly of the vehicle follows. This time, the participants follow the target process that has been worked out. Once again, the time is stopped and noted.
6. Another reflection takes place in the team. This time the following questions have to be answered and the answers written down on a flipchart:
   - What has changed compared to the first round?
   - Where are there limits to improvement? Why?
   - How can the experience from the simulation be used for everyday life? Are there any examples?

Challenge:	What is the quickest and easiest way to assemble the vehicle?
Task:	The circled vehicle is to be assembled so that it is roadworthy.
Roles in the game:	3 - 4 people for assembly and possibly 1 observer.

Fig. 7.5 Simulation with building blocks—initial situation

Closing

At the end of the simulation, the individual teams present their findings to the other groups. The discussion on the findings for everyday life and the experiences from the groups is particularly interesting.

Practical Tips

1. For the first attempt, it makes sense to follow the assembly instructions correctly, even if assembling it this way does not seem logical at times. Do not only measure the total time but also the times for the different steps. The times form the basis for the group to set an ambitious goal for the assembly, such as 30% less effort than in the current process.
2. Think about how many people will be involved in the assembly process and when, so that it is as efficient and effective as possible.
3. Be patient. It will not be possible to reduce the time needed for assembly by the desired 30% in the first round of improvements. Practice makes perfect. This also applies to continuous improvement.

7.1.3 Simulation 3: Simulation with Tennis Balls (Ball Point Game)

This simple simulation, which was developed by Boris Gloger® (2020), is ideal for familiarising participants with the agile approach to optimising processes in so-called sprints. The term 'sprint' comes from the Scrum method and stands for short, intensive runs that are repeated several times. The goal is to improve from one sprint to the next. This is done by defining measures to improve the process between the runs (Fig. 7.6).

Possible Applications/Benefits

This simulation is very suitable for activating participants at training events or seminars. For example, it is well suited for use after the lunch break. In a short time, the participants have an intensive experience of how processes can be continuously optimised, thanks to constant improvement. In my personal experience, the teams only get a few tennis balls through at the beginning. However, this changes after only two or three rounds. The improvements achieved result from the continuous review of the process and the implementation of targeted improvement measures.

However, this simulation is not only about conveying the effect of the improvement method but also about the experience of solving problems together as a team.

Carrying Out the Simulation

Preparation

The preparation is relatively simple. All you need to do is organise the following materials: 24 tennis balls, a basket and a clock to keep time.

Procedure

For the simulation, participants are given a basket with 24 tennis balls. The aim is to pass as many balls as possible through the row of participants within 1 minute and place them back in the same basket. The following rules must be adhered to:

- The participants form a team.
- The start and end points of the balls are identical.
- Each participant must touch each ball at least once.

Goal	
Practical experience to optimise processes in the team.	
Number of participants:	min. 6; max. 12
Time required:	around 30 minutes

Fig. 7.6 Simulation with tennis balls (ball point game)

Round	Estimate	Current	Deviation
1	10	25	+ 15
2	60	30	- 30
3	50	51	+ 1
4	60	74	+ 14
5	75	69	- 6
6	75	83	+ 8

Before each round, the participants estimate how many tennis balls they can pass through the row within one minute. This number is written on a flipchart as an estimate.

After each round, the number of tennis balls that reach the basket and the deviation from the previous estimate are written down.

A total of six rounds are completed, with two minutes between each round for optimisation.

Fig. 7.7 Evaluation simulation with tennis balls

- The ball must not be passed directly to the competitor next to it.
- The ball must be in the air for a short time during the handover ('airtime').
- If a tennis ball falls to the floor, it must not be picked up again.
- One round lasts 1 min. A total of six rounds are performed.
- Before the first run and between the individual runs, the team has 2 min each to prepare and optimise the process. The team also has to give an estimate for the next run.

Evaluation

The number of tennis balls worked through per round is recorded by the game leader as shown in Fig. 7.7.

When discussing the game balance after the last round, the participants report how satisfied they are with the result achieved and whether they would have expected this result at the beginning. Afterwards, the participants are asked to reflect on the following question:

- 'You played six rounds. You had a total of 12 minutes for "planning", that is, to think about your process method. If I had given you these 12 minutes of planning time *at the beginning of* the game and asked you: "Please devise a good plan of how you want to proceed!" – you think you would have achieved the same result that way too?'

The answer is regularly: 'No, we certainly wouldn't have achieved that. Only practical experience and continuous reflection, as well as the constant improvement of the process, have made this increase possible in the first place'.

Practical Tips

1. It happens that teams resign after three to four rounds. 'No more improvement is possible now'. In this case, it is advisable to suggest to the team to try two more rounds and to appoint a participant as

an 'observer'. This observer no longer plays, but watches from the outside and gives feedback to the team after each round – on the course of the simulation itself as well as on the discussion style and cooperation within the team.

2. It happens that one round gives a worse result than the previous round. In Fig. 7.7, this can be seen in the results of rounds 4 and 5. Here, an improvement measure was implemented that did not have the desired effect. In the final reflection, the answer is often that without this experience, the improvement could not have been realised in the next round.

Reference

Boris Gloger®. Retrieved on December 23, 2020., from https://www.borisgloger.com/wp-content/uploads/2016/08/Ball_Point_Game.pdf

Index

M. Hofmann, *A Holistic Approach to Process Optimisation*, Management for Professionals, https://doi.org/10.1007/978-3-658-34097-1

The manufacturer's authorised representative in the EU is Springer Nature Customer Service Centre GmbH, Europaplatz 3, 69115 Heidelberg, Germany. If you have any concerns regarding our products, please contact ProductSafety@springernature.com

Printed and bound by CPI Group (UK) Ltd, Croydon, CR0 4YY
30/09/2026
02225290-0001